Home Office Research Study 210

The extent and nature of stalking: findings from the 1998 British Crime Survey

Tracey Budd and Joanna Mattinson
with the assistance of Andy Myhill

Home Office Research, Development and Statistics Directorate
October 2000

Home Office Research Studies

The Home Office Research Studies are reports on research undertaken by or on behalf of the Home Office. They cover the range of subjects for which the Home Secretary has responsibility. Titles in the series are listed at the back of this report (copies are available from the address on the back cover). Other publications produced by the Research, Development and Statistics Directorate include Research Findings, the Research Bulletin, Statistical Bulletins and Statistical Papers.

The Research, Development and Statistics Directorate

RDS is part of the Home Office. The Home Office's purpose is to build a safe, just and tolerant society in which the rights and responsibilities of individuals, families and communities are properly balanced and the protection and security of the public are maintained.

RDS is also a part of the Government Statistical Service (GSS). One of the GSS aims is to inform Parliament and the citizen about the state of the nation and provide a window on the work and performance of government, allowing the impact of government policies and actions to be assessed.

Therefore -

Research Development and Statistics Directorate exists to improve policy making, decision taking and practice in support of the Home Office purpose and aims, to provide the public and Parliament with information necessary for informed debate and to publish information for future use.

"The views expressed in this report are those of the authors, not necessarily those of the Home Office (nor do they reflect Government policy)."

First published 2000
Application for reproduction should be made to the Communications and Development Unit, Room 201, Home Office, 50 Queen Anne's Gate, London SW1H 9AT.

Foreword

In recent years, stalking has increasingly been recognised as a social and legal problem. In England and Wales, the Protection from Harassment Act was introduced in 1997 to enable the criminal justice system to deal more effectively with cases of stalking and harassment. Despite this there has been relatively little research conducted to assess the extent or nature of the problem.

This report defines stalking as experiences of persistent and unwanted attention. It presents the findings from an innovative self-completion questionnaire included in the 1998 British Crime Survey. The report provides the first reliable, national level data on how frequently stalking occurs. It also identifies those most at risk and what types of behaviour victims are subjected to. The results will be of great interest to researchers and practitioners alike.

DAVID MOXON
Head of Crime and Criminal Justice Unit
Research, Development and Statistics Directorate

Acknowledgements

We are grateful to Sarah Partridge and Catriona Mirrlees-Black of the Home Office Research, Development and Statistics Directorate and Nina Stratford of the National Centre for Social Research who designed the self-completion questionnaire on which these findings are based. Thanks are also due to colleagues within RDS and Lorraine Sheridan (Leicester University) who provided valuable comments on early drafts and those who assisted in the preparation of the report for publication. Finally, we would like to thank all BCS respondents who agreed to complete the self-completion questionnaire.

Tracey Budd
Joanna Mattinson
Andy Myhill

Contents

The 1998 British Crime Survey included an innovative computerised self-completion questionnaire designed to provide the first reliable measure of the extent of 'stalking' in England and Wales. A nationally representative sample of 9,988 16 - to - 59 year-olds were asked whether they had been subject to 'persistent and unwanted attention' during their lifetime and during the preceding year. Those who had been subject to such incidents were asked details about their experience. The questionnaire was deliberately designed to capture a wide range of experiences that could potentially be regarded as incidents of stalking.

The extent of stalking

- Overall, 11.8 per cent of adults aged 16 to 59 could recall being subject to persistent and unwanted attention at some time in their lives. The figure was higher for women (16.1%) than men (6.8%). Three-quarters of those identified as being subject to persistent and unwanted attention were women.

- 2.9 per cent of adults aged 16 to 59 had been the subject of stalking in the 12 months prior to the interview. This equates to almost 0.9 million adults in England and Wales experiencing at least one episode of stalking during the previous year (0.61 million women and 0.27 million men had been victims).

- These figures are based on a very broad definition of stalking – 'persistent and unwanted attention' – which captures a wide range of experiences. Alternative estimates of stalking which proxy the two harassment offences created by the 1997 Protection from Harassment Act are given in Table 1.

Table 1: *Last year prevalence and estimated number of victims*

	Women	Men	All
Percent victims in last year			
Any persistent and			
unwanted attention	4.0	1.7	2.9
Distress or upset caused	3.7	1.3	2.6
Fear of violence	2.7	0.9	1.9
Best estimate of number of victims in last year (in millions)			
Any persistent and			
unwanted attention	0.61	0.27	0.88
Distress or upset caused	0.57	0.20	0.77
Fear of violence	0.41	0.14	0.55

Notes:
1. Source: 1998 British Crime Survey and ONS mid 1998 population estimates. The estimates are subject to sampling error.
3. Distress or upset are those incidents in which the victim was very, fairly or a little distressed.
4. Fear incidents are those in which the victim was threatened with violence, violence was used or the victim was very, fairly or a little afraid violence would be used

The victims

- Women were twice as likely as men to have experienced any persistent and unwanted attention in the last year (4.0% compared to 1.7%).

- Young women were particularly at risk. 16.8 per cent of women aged 16 to 19 and 7.8 per cent of those aged 20 to 24 recalled being subject to persistent and unwanted attention during the previous year. Risks were also high among women who were:
    - single
    - students
    - living in privately rented accommodation
    - living in a flat or maisonette
    - living in a lower income household.

- The nature of incidents experienced by men and women differed somewhat and key results are discussed below.

The offenders

- The majority (79%) of incidents involved only one perpetrator. Incidents against male victims were more likely to have involved more than one offender.

- Overall, eight in ten (81%) incidents reported to the survey were perpetrated by men. Male offenders were involved in 90 per cent of incidents against women, and 57 per cent of incidents against men.

- In 29 per cent of incidents the perpetrator had an intimate relationship with the victim (current or former spouse, partner, girl/boyfriend or date) at the beginning of the incident. Strangers were responsible in 34 per cent of incidents. The remaining incidents involved close friends, relatives, household members or acquaintances. Women were significantly more likely to be stalked by a stranger than male victims.

- Female victims were most likely to believe the perpetrator of the persistent and unwanted attention wanted to start or continue a relationship with them. Male victims were most likely to say the offender wished to annoy or upset them.

- The relatively high proportion of incidents against men perpetrated by men is particularly interesting. The majority of such incidents were committed by strangers (42%), though five per cent were carried out by a current or former partner. The most common reason given for male on male incidents was that the offender wished to upset or annoy the victim.

Experiences of stalking

- In about a third of cases reported to the survey the persistent and unwanted attention lasted less than a month, and in a further quarter (26%) between one and three months. However, for around one in five victims (19%) the persistent and unwanted attention lasted for a year or more. There were no differences between male and female victims.

- Experiences of persistent and unwanted attention were wide ranging. The most common experience was being forced into talking to the offender, with almost a half of all incidents (49%) involving this. Other relatively common experiences, reported in a third or more of incidents, were:
    - silent phone calls (45%)
    - being physically intimidated (42%)
    - being followed (39%)
    - being touched or grabbed (34%)
    - the offender waiting outside the victim's home (33%).

- Female victims were more likely to experience almost all of the types of stalking behaviour asked about. However, male victims were more likely to say the offender had threatened or actually used violence.

- The vast majority (78%) of victims had experienced more than one type of behaviour during their most recent episode. About a half of victims had been subjected to between two and five distinct types of behaviour and a further third to six or more. Women tended to experience more types of behaviour than men.

Impact upon the victims

- Ninety-two per cent of victims said they were very or fairly annoyed/irritated by their experience. Levels of distress or upset were lower, but still 75 per cent had found the experience very or fairly distressing/upsetting. Women were particularly likely to have been distressed or upset by their experience.

- Seventy-one per cent of those who had been the subject of persistent and unwanted attention said they had changed their behaviour in at least one of three ways. Fifty-nine per cent had avoided certain places or people, 35 per cent went out less than they had previously and 42 per cent started taking additional personal security measures. Seventy-six per cent of women had taken at least one of these measures compared to 59 per cent of men.

- Almost a third (31%) of victims were very or fairly afraid that violence would be used against them. A similar proportion (27%) were afraid violence would be used against a friend, relative or someone else they knew. Victims were less likely to fear a sexual offence, though 17 per cent did so.

Seeking help

- One-third of victims (33%) considered what had happened to be a crime and a further 37 per cent considered it to be 'wrong but not a crime'. A quarter felt it to be 'just something that happens'.

- Thirty-three per cent of victims said the police were aware of their most recent episode of persistent and unwanted attention. Sixty-one per cent of victims who reported the incident said they were satisfied with the way the police handled the matter. There were few differences between male and female victims.

- Four-fifths of victims (82%) stated they had told someone. Over half (55%) of all victims had told their spouse, partner, boyfriend or girlfriend, 72 per cent had confided in a friend, relative or neighbour, eight per cent had informed a doctor, social worker or carer. Women were more likely to tell someone about their experiences than men.

Chapter 1   Introduction

This report presents the findings from an innovative self-completion questionnaire included in the 1998 British Crime Survey (BCS) which was specifically designed to measure experiences of 'stalking'. The BCS findings provide the first reliable, national level picture of the extent and nature of stalking in England and Wales.

What is 'stalking'?

The term stalking acquired broad public recognition in Britain during the mid-1990s when a number of criminal cases were widely reported in the media in which the offender had repeatedly subjected his or her victim to either criminal behaviour or forms of harassment which fell short of being criminal.[1] The media labelled such incidents as stalking and the term quickly fell into popular usage. Prior to such cases, stalking tended to be viewed as a phenomenon of celebrity, with obsessive fans following or trying to contact their idols.

In response to the apparent growth in stalking (or certainly an increasing number of incidents coming to the attention of the criminal justice system), new legislation was introduced in England and Wales in 1997 to enable the criminal justice system to deal more effectively with such cases. The Protection From Harassment Act (1997) created two specific criminal offences to deal with the problem.[2] The first is the triable-either-way offence of putting people in fear of violence (Protection from Harassment Act 1997 Sec.4). The second is the summary offence of harassment (Protection from Harassment Act 1997 Sec.2). The higher level offence requires proof that the victim was put in fear of violence, regardless of whether or not the offender intended to do so, and attracts a maximum sentence of five years imprisonment. The lesser summary offence involves causing harassment or distress but does not require the victim to have been put in fear of violence, and attracts a maximum sentence of six months imprisonment. Again, the summary offence does not require the proof of intent on behalf of the offender.[3] For

---

1   A case in point is that of R v Burstow. Details of this case were publicised in the television documentary: "I'll Be Watching You" (Yorkshire Television, August 1999). Further details of the case are summarised in Harris (2000).

2   Prior to the Protection From Harassment Act (1997) criminal prosecution of 'stalkers' was possible under several disparate acts of Parliament depending on the type of offence which had been committed. For example, the Offences Against the Person Act (1861); the Public Order Act (1986); the Telecommunications Act (1984); Malicious Communications Act (1988); Matrimonial Homes Act (1983) and Domestic Violence and Matrimonial Proceedings Act (1976).

3   In 1998 there were 693 cautions and 2,221 convictions under the Protection from Harassment Act for the offence of harassment. For the offence of putting people in fear of violence there were 173 cautions and 522 convictions. Figures provided by Crime and Criminal Justice Unit (RDS), Home Office.

both offences conviction can result in a restraining order, breach of which carries a maximum penalty of five years imprisonment. In addition to the two criminal offences, the Protection From Harassment Act also created a statutory 'civil tort' which gives the victim the power to seek injunction and damages.

The Research, Development and Statistics Directorate of the Home Office has recently completed a research project undertaken to evaluate the effectiveness of the Protection From Harassment Act, including how the legislation is being used in practice by the police and the Crown Prosecution Service. The full findings are reported in Harris (2000). The main findings from the study are summarised in Appendix C.

Despite the recent legislation, the term stalking has no legal status in England and Wales and the types of behaviour that should be encompassed by the term remains contentious.[4] There are various definitions which could be adopted, forming a continuum from very narrow definitions to those which could potentially encompass a wide range of incidents. Definitions can vary in terms of the type and frequency of the behaviours included, the length of time over which they occur; and whether the intention of the perpetrator or the emotional, psychological or physical impact upon the victim are deemed relevant.

In the United States the legal definition of stalking varies widely from state to state, despite the development of a 'model' anti-stalking code by the National Institute of Justice.[5] Most states require the alleged stalker to have engaged in a 'course of conduct', usually defined as two or more acts, though what types of behaviour should be included and whether the perpetrator has to make a credible threat or not varies in the different statutes (Tjaden and Thoennes, 1998).

The National Violence Against Women Survey in the United States (see below for further details) employed the following definition, which closely follows the definition adopted in the 'model' anti-stalking code:

> *"a course of conduct directed at a specific person that involves repeated visual or physical proximity, non consensual communication, or verbal, written or implied threats, or a combination thereof, that would cause a reasonable person fear"* (Tjaden and Thoennes, 1998)

---

4   The Act, although informally referred to as 'anti-stalking law', does not actually use or define the term stalking. Rather it refers to a 'course of conduct' involving harassment on two or more occasions and states that 'References to harassing a person include alarming the person or causing the person distress' (s7(2)).

5   National Criminal Justice Association, Project to Develop a Model Anti-Stalking Code for States, Washington D. C.: U.S. Department of Justice, National Institute of Justice, October 1993.

This definition does not require perpetrators to have made a credible threat of violence against the victim, but does require victims to either have been very frightened or to have feared bodily harm.

There are many other definitions of stalking that have been offered by various commentators. Many describe the types of incident which could be included, on the basis of the frequency of events and/or the impact on the victim, rather than specifying a definitive list of behaviours that constitute stalking behaviour.[6]

Previous research

Research into stalking is in its infancy. The majority of studies undertaken to date have been relatively small in scale, involving unrepresentative or clinical samples to explore in depth the nature of stalking victimisation, the impact upon the victim or the motivation of offenders. Most of these studies have been conducted in the United States or Australia (see for example, Hall (1998); Roberts and Dziegielewski (1996); Nicastro et al. (2000); Meloy, (1998); Pathé and Mullen (1997); Mullen et al. (2000)).

In this country there have been relatively few, even small-scale studies though Farnham et al. (2000) conducted a study of 50 'stalkers', identified from case files from a regional forensic service, and concluded that:

> "the greatest danger of serious violence from stalkers in the UK is not from strangers or from people with psychotic illness, but from non-psychotic ex-partners".

Although these small-scale research studies are invaluable in helping to illuminate the context in which victimisation occurs and the effects at the individual level, it is also important to assess the extent and nature of the problem at a national level. Only large-scale quantitative surveys based on representative samples can achieve this. Such surveys are extremely costly and resource intensive and therefore it is perhaps not surprising that few such studies have been previously undertaken – the National Violence Against Women (NVAW) Survey in the United States being the most comprehsive.[7] The NVAW Survey (see page 2 for the definition of stalking used) concluded that:

6   See for example, Wallis (1996); Pathé and Mullen (1997); Wright et al. (1996); Coleman (1997); Campbell (1997/8) and Marston and Thompson (1997).

7   Despite its name the NVAW Survey also covered men. Telephone interviews were conducted with a representative sample of 8,000 men and 8,000 women between November 1995 and May 1996. The Australian Bureau of Statistics conducted a national survey which included questions on stalking in 1996 (Australian Bureau of Statistics, 1996). However, this only covered women being stalked by men.

"Stalking is more prevalent than previously thought: 8 per cent of women and 2 per cent of men in the United States have been stalked at some time in their life" (Tjaden and Thoennes, 1998).

Details of the NVAW Survey and how it compares to the BCS are given in Appendix D.

The most significant prevalence study undertaken in this country explored the experiences of 348 women who were members of the trade union Unison (Sheridan et al., forthcoming). The study concluded that 82 respondents (24% of the sample) had experienced at least one episode of stalking in their lifetime.[8] Although this study provides an indication of the prevalence of stalking among a specific sub-group of women, the results are unlikely to reflect those of all adult women in the population. Furthermore, the sample excluded men and so provides no information about male victimisation.

The British Crime Survey stalking self-completion questionnaire

The British Crime Survey stalking self-completion module provides the first reliable, national level data to address the following important questions:

- How prevalent is stalking in England and Wales?

- Who are the victims of stalking?

- Who are the perpetrators of stalking and, in particular, what type of prior relationship did they have with their victim?

- What types of stalking behaviour do victims experience?

- What impact do experiences of stalking have upon victims?

---

8   This paper-and-pencil self-completion study presented respondents with a list of 42 behaviours defined as intrusive acts and asked them (a) which behaviours they considered to be examples of stalking and (b) to report which behaviours they had ever experienced. Those who had experienced at least one incident were asked to describe the worst incident in detail. Expert raters assessed whether these experiences constituted an episode of stalking, defined as 'a series of actions directed at one individual by another which, taken as a whole, amount to unwanted persistent personal harassment', and concluded that 82 women had experienced at least one incident (a prevalence figure of 24%). Raters also assessed whether the incidents could, in theory, be prosecutable under the Protection From Harassment Act, concluding that this was so in 115 cases (33% of the original 348).

The information provided by British Crime Survey will be important in informing the development and implementation of policy with regard to stalking. The findings with the greatest policy implications are discussed in Chapter 8.

The British Crime Survey

The British Crime Survey (BCS) is a large, nationally representative survey of adults aged 16 and over living in private households in England and Wales. The main purpose of the survey is to measure the extent of criminal victimisation in England and Wales, though it also covers a wide range of other crime related issues (Mirrlees-Black et al., 1998). To date the BCS has been carried out eight times.[9] The main part of the survey is conducted as a face-to-face interview, but since 1992 the survey has also included self-completion modules on particularly sensitive topics for respondents to complete following the interview.[10]

The stalking self-completion module

The 1998 British Crime Survey is the only sweep that has included a self-completion module on stalking.[11] Self-completion methods offer the most confidential means of collecting survey information and encourage people to report experiences which they may be reluctant to divulge in a face-to-face interview. The questionnaire was implemented using a laptop computer (a method known as CASI – Computer Assisted Self-Interviewing). Only respondents aged 16 to 59 were asked to complete the self-completion module. In total 9,988 of those eligible completed the questionnaire. The overall response rate was 76 per cent (the response rate for the face-to-face interview element of the survey was 79%, and 97% of those eligible completed the self-completion module). Further details on the methodology are reported in Appendix E.

---

9 There were sweeps in 1982, 1984, 1988, 1992, 1994, 1996 and 1998. The most recent sweep was conducted in 2000. The next sweep will be in 2001. The BCS covered Scotland as well as England and Wales in the first and third sweeps (1982 and 1988) hence the name British Crime Survey. Since then crime surveys have been separately conducted in Scotland (in 1993, 1996 and 2000). There have also been surveys in Northern Ireland (in 1994 and 1998).

10 Other than stalking, there have been self-completion modules on drug misuse (Mott and Mirrlees-Black, 1995; Ramsay and Partridge, 1999; Ramsay and Spiller, 1997; Ramsay and Percy, 1996); domestic violence (Mirrlees-Black, 1999); sexual victimisation (Percy and Mayhew, 1997) and handling stolen goods (Sutton, 1998).

11 In the 1982 and 1992 BCS there was a module in the face-to-face interview which measured experiences of obscene or offensive telephone calls (see Buck et al., 1995).

The questionnaire was deliberately designed to capture a wide range of experiences that could potentially be defined as stalking. Respondents were asked if, since the age of 16, they had ever been subject to 'persistent and unwanted attention', whether from somebody they knew or a stranger. The BCS definition of stalking depends on only two elements. First, that the behaviours experienced were not desired by the victim and second, that they recurred over an unspecified period of time. Unlike the definition adopted by Tjaden and Thoennes (see page 2), the BCS definition does not require victims to have experienced fear.

Persistent and unwanted attention was described to respondents at the beginning of the questionnaire in the following way:

> "People may sometimes be pestered or harassed either by someone they know or a stranger. This person might do things like phoning or writing, following them or waiting outside their home or workplace."

The description was designed to provide some examples of the types of behaviour that could constitute 'persistent and unwanted attention', rather than a definitive list of all behaviours within the definition. The BCS measure is entirely dependent upon respondents' interpretations of the term 'persistent and unwanted attention' and whether they feel they have been subject to any such behaviour. Measurement issues are further discussed in Appendix E.

The full self-completion questionnaire is at Appendix F.

Structure of the report

Chapter 2 reports on the extent of stalking in England and Wales. Two main measures are discussed: lifetime prevalence and prevalence of stalking in the previous year.

Chapter 3 explores how the risk of being subject to stalking varies across different groups of the population.

Chapter 4 provides information about the perpetrators of stalking incidents, including whether they had any prior relationship with their victim. The chapter also introduces a typology of stalking based on the victim/offender relationship. The typology is used throughout the remainder of the report.

Chapter 5 examines in some detail the nature of stalking incidents, in particular the types of behaviours involved in episodes of stalking and the period of time over which the incidents occurred.

Chapter 6 looks at the impact of stalking upon the victims, in terms of both emotional reactions and lifestyle changes.

Chapter 7 examines what type of support and advice victims seek, including whether the police were informed about the incident.

Chapter 8 concludes with a discussion of the key findings and the implications they have for policy.

Chapter 2   The extent of stalking

This chapter provides national level estimates of the prevalence of stalking, defined as persistent and unwanted attention, against those aged 16 to 59 in England and Wales.[12] Both lifetime and last year prevalence figures are given. Respondents were asked if they had ever been the subject of persistent and unwanted attention since the age of 16, and, if so, if they had experienced such attention in the last year.

The lifetime measure provides an indication of the number of adults who have been the subject of stalking at some time since the age of 16 and provides an appropriate means of identifying victims and non-victims. In contrast, the last year measure indicates the current extent of the problem, which is invaluable in policy development, but is less appropriate for differentiating victims and non-victims because only recent victimisation is included.

Both measures are likely to underestimate the true prevalence of persistent and unwanted attention because respondents may not recall incidents or may be unwilling to report their experiences to the survey. The lifetime measure will be more susceptible to recall problems because people are less likely to remember events further back in time. Furthermore, because less serious incidents are more likely to be forgotten, the lifetime measure will tend to be biased towards more serious incidents.[13] For a fuller discussion of these issues see Appendix E.

Lifetime prevalence

Overall, just over one in ten (11.8%) adults aged 16 to 59 recalled being the subject of persistent and unwanted attention on at least one occasion since the age of 16. The figure was much higher for women than men. 16.1 per cent of women had experienced persistent and unwanted attention at some time in their life, compared to 6.8 per cent of men. Three-quarters (73%) of all those identified as being subject to persistent and unwanted attention were women.

---

12 Throughout this report the term stalking is used to refer to incidents of persistent and unwanted attention, unless otherwise stated. Chapter 1 discusses the definition of 'persistent and unwanted attention'. For the exact questions see Appendix F.

13 This bias is also likely to apply, though to a lesser extent, to last year estimates.

14 In 81 incidents reported to the survey the victim had been living in the same household as the perpetrator during the entire period in which the persistent and unwanted attention occurred. These respondents were not asked subsequent questions about the nature of their experiences and so have been excluded from all analysis presented in this report. Including the 81 cases does not change the lifetime prevalence figure.

Among both women and men, those who were younger were more likely to have experienced persistent and unwanted attention, although they would have had less time in which to do so (Figure 2.1, Table A2.1). Almost a quarter of women aged 16 to 19 and a fifth aged 20 to 29 reported experiencing persistent and unwanted attention, compared to a tenth of women aged 55 to 59. Among men, those aged 20 to 24 were most at risk.

Figure 2.1: *Lifetime (since the age of 16) prevalence, by age and sex*

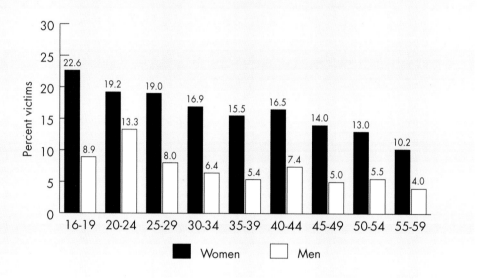

There are several possible explanations for this pattern:

- First, the results could reflect reality in that stalking is primarily an experience of younger people and there has been a real increase in stalking over time.

- Second, if stalking is primarily an experience of younger people, then older people will have to recall experiences from longer ago. As already discussed people are less likely to remember incidents further back in time.

- Third, older people may have a narrower definition of what constitutes persistent and unwanted attention than younger people or may be more inhibited about revealing their experiences in the survey context.

It is likely that all three of these factors play at least some role in accounting for the results.

Last year prevalence

Exactly a quarter of those who had experienced persistent and unwanted attention said that some of this had taken place during the previous year.[15] This equates to 2.9 per cent of all adults aged 16 to 59 being the subject of such behaviour in the last year. Overall, risks were higher for women (4.0%) than men (1.7%). This is due to the particularly high risks among younger women. 16.8 per cent of women aged 16 to 19 and 7.8 per cent of those aged 20 to 24 reported having been stalked in the last year (Figure 2.2, Table A2.2). Among men in these age groups the respective figures were 3.1 per cent and 4.6 per cent. There was little difference in risks for men and women aged 40 or over.

Figure 2.2: Last year prevalence by age and sex

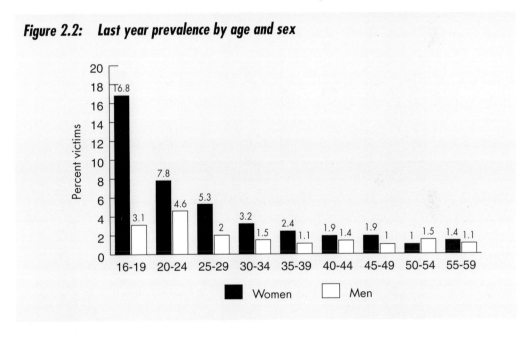

The high risk among young women is particularly striking, though it is difficult to assess to what degree this reflects real differences and to what degree this reflects response biases. It may be that young women are more likely to define experiences as constituting persistent and unwanted attention. These issues are further discussed in Chapter 3.

---

15 The last year prevalence question asked about experience over the 12 months prior to the interview. Because interviews took place between January and June 1998 the recall period varies depending on the date of interview. For example, for interviews which took place in March 1998, the respondent was asked whether any of the persistent and unwanted attention had taken place since March 1997.

Number of victims

The BCS estimates that in 1998 there were 3.53 million adults aged 16 to 59 in England and Wales who had experienced persistent and unwanted attention at some time since the age of 16. This included 0.88 million who had been victimised in the last year.[16]

Figure 2.3 gives the estimates for men and women separately. Almost two and a half million women had been the subject of persistent and unwanted attention at some time since the age of 16, with 0.61 million experiencing an incident in the last year. The figures for men were far lower at 1.07 million and 0.27 million respectively.

These figures appear to be relatively high. However, it should be borne in mind that they are based on a very broad definition of stalking – experiences of 'persistent and unwanted attention'. Within this there will be a wide range of experiences, varying in terms of the types of behaviour experienced, the length over which they occurred and the emotional impact upon the victim. Alternative estimates of stalking are discussed below.

Figure 2.3:   **Number of victims of persistent and unwanted attention in England and Wales – last year and lifetime (since the age of sixteen) estimates**

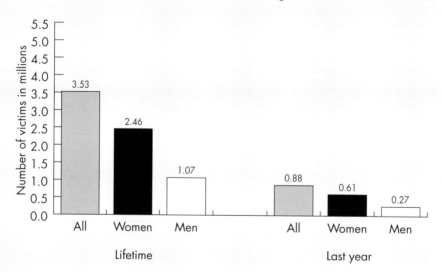

---

16   Estimates of the number of adults in the country who have been subject to persistent and unwanted attention are derived by multiplying prevalence rates by the total number of adults aged 16 to 59 in England and Wales in 1998.

Figure 2.3 presents the 'best' estimates of the number of victims. Because the estimates are based on a sample of the population, they are subject to sampling error and may differ to the true number of victims in the population. Table 2.1 shows the best estimates and the range within which there is 95 per cent chance that the true figures lie. For example, there is 95 per cent chance that the true number of female victims in the last year lies between 0.52 million and 0.71 million. Sampling error is further discussed in Appendix E.

Table 2.1: Number of victims of persistent and unwanted attention in England and Wales - last year and lifetime estimates

	Best estimate (millions)	Lowest estimate (millions)	Highest estimate (millions)
Lifetime estimate	3.53	3.21	3.85
Women	2.46	2.28	2.64
Men	1.07	0.93	1.21
Last year estimate	0.88	0.71	1.05
Women	0.61	0.52	0.71
Men	0.27	0.19	0.34

Notes:
1. Source: 1998 British Crime Survey and ONS mid 1998 population estimates.
2. The estimates are subject to sampling error. The lowest and highest estimates are based on 95% confidence intervals and assume a design effect of 1.2.

Alternative estimates

The estimates presented above are based on a relatively broad definition of stalking – 'persistent and unwanted attention'. The BCS self-completion questionnaire asked those who had been the subject of such attention detailed questions about the nature of their most recent episode[17] and it is therefore possible to adjust the definition in various ways to produce alternative 'last year' estimates.[18]

---

17 The term episode refers to a period of persistent and unwanted attention carried out by the same offender, not simply the last occurrence of any such behaviour within the episode.
18 The detailed questions about experiences of 'persistent and unwanted attention' pertain to the most recent episode. In some cases victims may have experienced several episodes. This means that prevalence estimates based on definitions derived from last episode details will be underestimates – though the impact is likely to be small.

Here we will only consider definitions that provide the closest approximation to the types of incident that could potentially be prosecutable under the Protection from Harassment Act (1997). As discussed in Chapter 1, the Act does not tightly define what would constitute harassment although it does state that harassing a person can include alarming the person or causing them distress. Furthermore, the Act created two offences: the summary offence of causing harassment or distress and the higher level offence of putting people in fear of violence.

Restricting the BCS definition to incidents of persistent and unwanted attention that caused the victim upset or distress results in a last year prevalence estimate of 2.6 per cent. This equates to a 'best' estimate of 0.77 million victims. Restricting the definition to those episodes which involved violence or the threat of violence or in which the victim was fearful violence would be used against them gives a prevalence estimate of 1.9 per cent (0.55 million victims).

Table 2.2 summarises the last year prevalence figures and 'best' estimates of the total number of victims for the various definitions of stalking.

Table 2.2: Last year prevalence and estimated number of victims

	Women	Men	All
Percent victims in last year			
Any persistent and unwanted attention	4.0	1.7	2.9
Distress or upset caused	3.7	1.3	2.6
Fear of violence	2.7	0.9	1.9
Best estimate of number of victims in last year (in millions)			
Any persistent and unwanted attention	0.61	0.27	0.88
Distress or upset caused	0.57	0.20	0.77
Fear of violence	0.41	0.14	0.55

Notes:
1. Source: 1998 British Crime Survey and ONS mid 1998 population estimates.
2. The estimates are subject to sampling error. Table A2.3 in Appendix A gives the 95 per cent confidence intervals on the distress and fear estimates.
3. Distress or upset are those incidents in which the victim was very, fairly or a little distressed.
4. Fear incidents are those in which the victim was threatened with violence, violence was used or the victim was very, fairly or a little afraid violence would be used.

The remainder of this report examines incidents that fall under the broadest definition of stalking – persistent and unwanted attention. Chapters 5 and 6 discuss the types of behaviours experienced in episodes of persistent and unwanted attention and the impact such incidents have upon the victims.

This chapter examines how the risk of being subject to persistent and unwanted attention varies across different socio-demographic groups. First, the results presented in Chapter 2 on the variation in risk by age and sex are discussed, then other socio-demographic factors are considered.

The analysis is restricted to last year victimisation because the socio-demographic characteristics are those which applied at the time of the interview. It would be inappropriate to link current measures to lifetime risk because many of the characteristics, such as employment status, change over time and may not have applied at the time of victimisation.[19] Furthermore, it is more informative to be able to identify those currently at high risk.

The results presented in this chapter are based on bivariate analysis which takes each risk factor in turn. The results indicate which characteristics are associated with an increased risk of victimisation, not which characteristics cause increased risk. Many of the characteristics overlap to some degree and it is difficult to assess the unique contribution of each.

It is also important to recognise that definitions of persistent and unwanted attention and willingness to report incidents to the survey may differ across social groups. If such systematic response differences do exist, they will to some degree account for apparent differences in risk estimates.

Finally, it should be noted that given the relative rarity of last year victimisation – a national prevalence figure of only 2.9 per cent – it is quite difficult to detect significant variation in risk across different social groups. Throughout this chapter where differences are referred to as significant this is at the 10 per cent significance level (i.e. there is only a 10 per cent chance that the observed difference could be solely due to sampling variation). Table A3.1 in Appendix A gives the prevalence risks for all of the groups considered in this chapter and indicates where the risks are significantly higher than the national average.

---

19 It should be noted that restricting the analysis to last year victimisation does not completely avoid this problem as some of the victims' circumstances may still have changed following their victimisation.

Risk factors

Age and sex

As reported in Chapter 2, 4.0 per cent of women said that they had experienced persistent and unwanted attention during the last year, compared to 1.7 per cent of men. Young women were particularly at risk with 16.8 per cent of women aged between 16 and 19 reporting an incident to the survey.

It is possible that these patterns are, at least in part, accounted for by differences in how men and women, and particularly young women, interpret both the term persistent and unwanted attention and their own experiences.

Thus, it may be that women are more likely to regard incidents as constituting persistent and unwanted attention and more likely to think their own experiences warrant reporting in a crime survey.[20] Women may feel more threatened by their experiences because they are more alert to the risks of violence, including sexual violence, or because in the majority of incidents against them the perpetrator is male (see Chapter 4) and on average physically stronger than themselves. Chapter 6 does show that women subjected to persistent and unwanted attention are more fearful of violence, including sexual assault, than male victims.

Marital status

Risks of victimisation were highest among those who described their marital status as single, never married (6.7%), followed by those who described themselves as separated (5.1%) or divorced (4.2%). Figures were lowest for those who were married (1.2%) or widowed (1.6%).

This general pattern held for both men and women (Table 3.1). However, whereas among women those who were single, separated, divorced or cohabiting were all significantly more likely to be victims than those who were married, among men only those who were single were significantly more at risk than their married counterparts.

---

20 The crime survey context is further discussed in Appendix E.

Table 3.1: Last year prevalence, by sex and marital status

Percent victims	Women	Men	All
Marital status			
Single	9.8	3.7	6.7
Separated	6.7	1.9	5.1
Divorced	5.8	1.4	4.2
Cohabiting	4.6	1.0	3.0
Widowed	2.1	-	1.6
Married	1.4	1.1	1.2
All	4.0	1.7	2.9

Notes:
1. Source: 1998 British Crime Survey.
2. - indicates no respondents in this category were victims.

Employment status

Risks were highest among those who classified themselves as students.[21] Overall, eight per cent of students said they had experienced persistent or unwanted attention in the last year. Among female students the figure was 12.4 per cent and among male students 3.0 per cent. Those who were classified as unemployed also had relatively high risks. This was particularly so among women, with 7.1 per cent of unemployed women reporting an episode to the survey (Table 3.2).

Table 3.2: Last year prevalence, by sex and employment status

Percent victims	Women	Men	All
Employment status			
Student	12.4	3.0	8.0
Unemployed	7.1	2.1	4.0
Employed	3.6	1.7	2.6
At home	2.8	-	2.7
Retired	0.8	-	0.5
All	4.0	1.7	2.9

Notes:
1. Source: 1998 British Crime Survey.
2. Students are those who consider themselves to be full-time students (see footnote 21).
3. - incidates no respondents in this category were victims.

21 Those defined as students only include those who were not in paid work in the seven days before interview and considered themselves to be full-time students.

Educational level

Risks of victimisation were lowest for those without any educational qualifications (1.7%). Those whose highest held qualification was A-level or equivalent were most at risk (3.8%), followed by those with GCSE or equivalent qualifications (3.5%). However, those for whom the highest qualification was a first degree, postgraduate degree or equivalent were not particularly at risk, at 2.8 per cent being close to the national average.

This pattern differs slightly for men and women. Among men there is little difference in risk by educational level, while among women risks do vary, with those with A-level or equivalent qualifications most at risk (Figure 3.1). The below average risks among women with degree level qualifications is likely to reflect the fact that risks are highest among those aged between 16 and 19 (i.e. before degree level qualifications can generally be obtained).

Figure 3.1: Last year prevalence, by sex and educational attainment

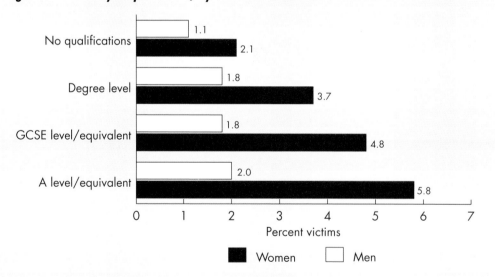

Household income

Overall, those living in lower income households were more likely to have experienced persistent and unwanted attention during the last year. 4.5% of those in households with an income of less than £15,000 per annum had been victims, compared to 2.2 per cent of those in higher income households.

Figure 3.2 shows the results for men and women. Among both men and women those living in households with an annual income of less than £15,000 were significantly more at risk than those in more affluent households.

Figure 3.2:   Last year prevalence, by sex and household income

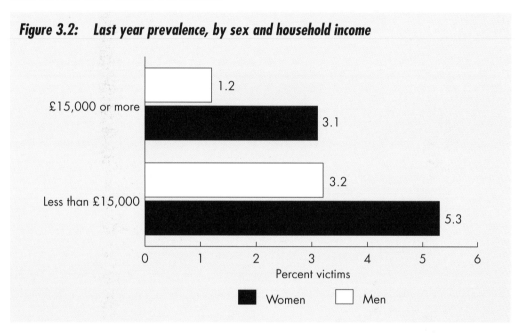

Dwelling and tenure type

Overall, those living in privately rented accommodation were most likely to report an episode of persistent and unwanted attention (4.8%), followed by those in Local Authority or Housing Association properties (4.3%). Among homeowners the figure was significantly lower at 2.1 per cent.

The pattern differed somewhat for men and women (Figure 3.3). Among women, private renters were at highest risk, though those renting from a Local Authority or Housing Association were also significantly more at risk than those living in owner-occupied dwellings. Among men, only those in Local Authority or Housing Association accommodation were significantly more at risk than owner-occupiers.

Figure 3.3: Last year prevalence, by sex and tenure

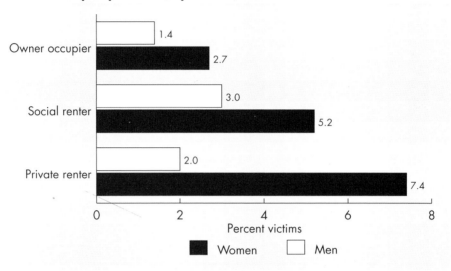

In terms of dwelling type, those living in flats or maisonettes were at greatest risk, with 4.8 per cent experiencing an incident in the previous year, followed by those living in terraced (3.1%) or semi-detached (2.9%) housing. Risks were lowest among those in detached houses at 1.9 per cent.

The patterns do differ to some degree for men and women, though among both men and women flat dwellers were most at risk (Figure 3.4).

Figure 3.4: Last year prevalence, by sex and dwelling type

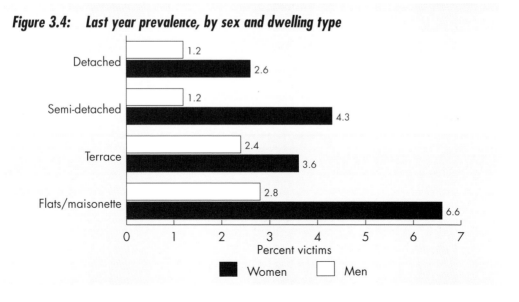

Area

Those living in inner city or urban areas were most at risk, with 3.2 per cent experiencing persistent and unwanted attention in the previous year. In rural areas, the figure was significantly lower at 2.1 per cent.

Among both men and women risks were higher in inner city or urban areas than rural areas, though the difference was not significant among women (Figure 3.5).

Table A3.2, Appendix A, gives prevalence risk estimates by Government Office Region.

Figure 3.5: *Last year prevalence, by sex and area type*

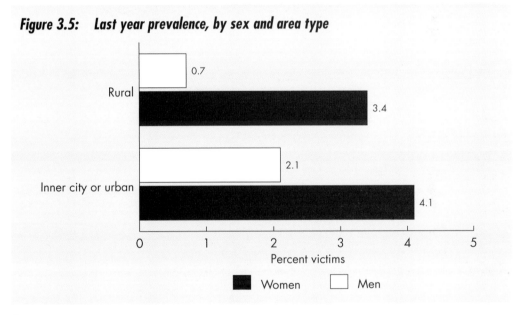

Summary

Regardless of the social characteristic under consideration women were invariably more at risk of persistent and unwanted attention than men. Risks were particularly high among the following groups of women – those who were:
- aged between 16 and 24
- single
- students
- living in privately rented accommodation
- living in a flat or a maisonette
- living in low income households (less than £15,000 per annum).

The analysis presented in this chapter has indicated which groups of women are most at risk, but because many of the risk factors overlap it is difficult to assess the unique contribution of each characteristic. For example, students are likely to be young and single. Multivariate analysis techniques would be required to assess which particular characteristics are most important in influencing risk.

Chapter 4 {style="display:inline"} The offenders

This chapter first provides some details about the perpetrators of stalking incidents, their sex and age and their relationship to the victim. A typology of stalking is then discussed based on the gender of the victim and their relationship with the offender.[22] This typology is used throughout Chapters 5, 6 and 7.

In total 1,262 respondents said they had been subject to at least one episode of persistent and unwanted attention at some time since the age of 16, including 313 cases where an episode had taken place in the last year. All those who had experienced stalking behaviour were asked a series of detailed questions about what happened, including the characteristics of the perpetrator.[23] Respondents who had experienced more than one episode were asked questions with respect to the most recent, though it is possible that some of those who had experienced more than one episode decided to report on the most 'serious', or even reported details from more than one episode.[24]

The results presented in this and the following chapters are based on all incidents reported to the survey, regardless of whether they occurred in the last year or not.[25]

Number of offenders

In the majority of episodes (79%) reported to the survey the stalking was carried out by one person alone.[26] Nine per cent of episodes involved two people, four per cent three people and eight per cent four or more. Interestingly, men were less likely to be victims of single offender incidents (66%) than women (84%). In fact, a fifth (20%) of incidents against men involved three or more offenders (Figure 4.1). This pattern suggests that the nature of incidents against men and women is rather different, an issue which is explored further in this and the following chapters.

---

22 The term offender is used to refer to the person who the victim thought was responsible for the stalking. It is not used in the legal sense of someone found guilty of committing the offence.

23 As stated in Chapter 2, footnote 14, incidents in which the victim and offender had been living together throughout the entire episode of persistent and unwanted attention have been excluded from all analysis.

24 Although a question was included to assess whether victims had experienced more than one episode of persistent and unwanted attention, an error in the computer program means that this data is not available for analysis. It is therefore impossible to determine how many victims had experienced more than one episode of persistent and unwanted attention.

25 The term incidents is also used to refer to an episode of stalking in which the victim experienced 'persistent and unwanted attention'.

26 In 65 cases (5% of incidents) the victim did not know the number of people responsible for the persistent and unwanted attention. These cases have been excluded from the base.

Figure 4.1: Number of offenders, by sex of victim

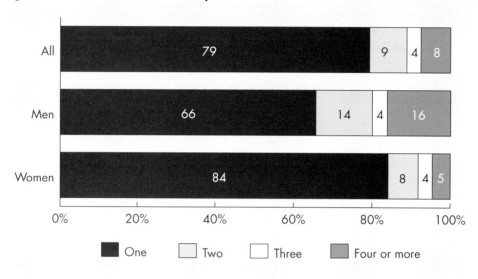

Age and sex of offenders

Victims of persistent and unwanted attention were asked for information about the age and sex of the perpetrator. For the 21 per cent of episodes that involved more than one perpetrator the respondent was asked to provide details about just one of the offenders.[27]

Overall, just over eight in ten (81%) incidents were perpetrated by men, with a half (51%) of incidents involving men aged between 20 and 39 years of age (Table A4.1).

However, the age and sex distribution of perpetrators in incidents against men and women varied considerably. In the vast majority (90%) of incidents committed against women the offender was male (Table A4.1). Offenders in incidents against men were more evenly distributed – 57 per cent were committed by men and 43 per cent by women. Incidents against men were also more likely to involve young offenders. Just over a third (37%) involved someone under the age of 20, compared to less than a fifth (17%) of incidents against women.

---

27 This was the main person involved, unless the victim was unable to identify any one of a group of offenders as being mainly responsible, in which case they were asked to select just one person to talk about.

Despite the different stalking definition, the National Violence Against Women Survey conducted in the United States (see Chapter 1 for further details) produced similar results with 94 per cent of stalking incidents against women and 60 per cent against men being committed by male offenders (Tjaden and Thoennes, 1998).

The relationship between offender and victim

The survey asked victims of stalking what type of relationship they had with the offender at the time the persistent and unwanted attention began. The questions were detailed and the full results are reported in Table A4.2 in Appendix A.

Overall, almost two-thirds of stalking incidents involved a perpetrator previously known to the victim in some way. Twenty-nine per cent of incidents were committed by someone who was in an intimate relationship (defined as spouse, partner, boyfriend/girlfriend or date) with the victim at the start of the episode of persistent and unwanted attention, or by a former intimate. A further third (32%) were committed by an acquaintance of the victim (including 9% involving a manager/colleague at work or member of the public contacted through work)[28]; six per cent were committed by a close friend, relative or other household member. A third (34%) of incidents were committed by someone the victim did not know in any way prior to the incident.

Figure 4.2 gives the results for male and female victims separately. The pattern is on the whole very similar, though women were significantly more likely to have been victims of stranger incidents than men (significant at 10% level).

The National Violence Against Women Survey in the United States similarly reported that the majority of incidents were committed by someone known to the victim in some way (Tjaden and Thoennes, 1998). However, unlike the BCS, the US survey found men were more likely to be victims of a stranger incident than women (36% as opposed to 23%), while women were far more likely to be stalked by current or former intimates than men (59% as opposed to 30%). The difference in results is likely to be at least in part due to the different definitions of stalking used in the two surveys (see Chapter 1 and Appendix D for details).

---

28 A proportion of the acquaintance incidents may have involved neighbours. Unfortunately, this option was not offered on the questionnaire so it is not possible to ascertain how common this type of incident was.

Figure 4.2: Offender's relationship to the victim

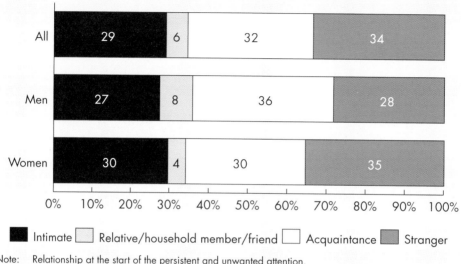

Note: Relationship at the start of the persistent and unwanted attention.

Victims who said that the perpetrator was someone other than a current or former spouse or a stranger were asked how well they knew the offender (well, casually or just by sight) at the start of the persistent and unwanted attention. In 40 per cent of episodes the victim said they had known the offender well and in a further 46 per cent they had know the offender casually. The full results are given in Table A4.3.

Reasons for stalking

The BCS asked victims of persistent and unwanted attention why they thought the perpetrator paid them such attention. Different questions were asked depending on the victim's prior relationship with the perpetrator (see Appendix F).[29]

The questions are quite limited and a relatively large proportion of respondents gave 'other' as the reason for the episode of stalking[30] The results, nonetheless, provide some indication of the motives of offenders. The most common reasons given were the perpetrator wished to start a relationship (22%), the offender wanted to annoy or upset the victim (16%) or the offender wished to continue a relationship (12%).

---

29 Unfortunately, due to a routing error those who said the perpetrator was their husband/wife at the start of the persistent and unwanted attention were asked the incorrect question (stk2reas rather than stk1reas). This though only affects a small number of cases.

30 21% offered 'other' as a reason. Unfortunately, due to the nature of the CASI questionnaire we do not know what respondents were thinking of when they gave 'other' as their answer. A further 20% said don't know.

Women were more likely than men to say the offender wanted to start or continue a relationship. Among men the most common reason given was that the offender wanted to annoy or upset them (Figure 4.3).

Figure 4.3: *Most common reasons for stalking*

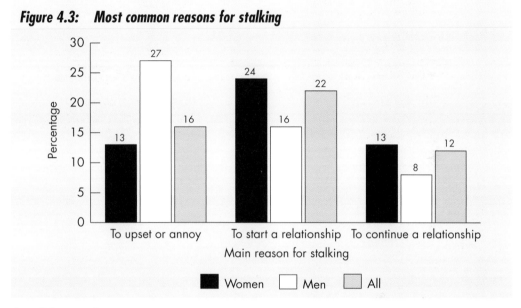

A stalking typology

In reporting results on violent crime, the British Crime Survey has adopted a typology of violence based on the relationship between the victim and the offender. This is primarily to aid the development of appropriate policy responses. Three types of violence are identified on this basis: stranger violence, acquaintance violence, and domestic violence (Mirrlees-Black et al., 1996; Mirrlees-Black, 1999).[31]

In the same way, it is useful to distinguish episodes of stalking on the basis of the prior relationship between the victim and the perpetrator. The results reported above indicate that there are three main relationship types, each accounting for about a third of incidents: intimate, acquaintance and stranger. Table A4.4 in Appendix A shows the prevalence risks of these three stalking types, for men and women separately, on a lifetime and last year basis. Relatives, close friends and other household members have been included in the intimate grouping.[32]

---

31 Violence includes common assaults and woundings. In addition there is a fourth type of violence, mugging, which comprises all incidents of robbery or snatch thefts.

32 Relatives, close friends and other household members were included in the intimate group on the basis that in the majority of these incidents the victim knows the offender very well. In contrast, those who fall into the acquaintance group are usually only known casually or by sight.

The stalking typology adopted in the remainder of this report is based on both the victim/offender relationship and the sex of the victim and comprises the following four groups:[33]

- Female victim – intimate relationship with the offender
- Female victim – non-intimate relationship with the offender
- Male victim – intimate relationship with the offender
- Male victim – non-intimate relationship with the offender.

The non-intimate group includes both stranger and acquaintance incidents. Box 4.1 summarises the relationships included in the intimate and non-intimate groupings. Table A4.5 in Appendix A shows the detailed relationship breakdown for intimate and non-intimate incidents for men and women. Intimate incidents against men were more likely to involve friends, relatives or other household members than such incidents against women. Similarly, the majority of non-intimate incidents against men involved an acquaintance, whereas among women non-intimate incidents were more likely to involve a stranger.

Box 4.1:   *Intimate and non-intimate definitions*

Intimate	Non-intimate
Spouse or former spouse	Stranger
Partner or former partner	Casual acquaintance
Boy/girlfriend or former boy/girlfriend	Manager/employer or colleague at work
Date	Member of public contacted through work
Relative	Other known person
Other household member	
Close friend	

Overall, 4.1 per cent of adults had experienced an intimate stalking episode at some time in their life, and 7.7 per cent a non-intimate incident. On a last year basis the figures were 1.1 per cent and 1.8 per cent respectively. Regardless of the relationship with the offender women were more than twice at risk than men (Figure 4.4).

---

33 The typology developed included sex of the victim in addition to the victim/offender relationship because preliminary analysis indicated that the experiences of men and women differed markedly, both in terms of the types of behaviour experienced and the consequences. Due to the relatively small number of incidents against men it was not possible to use a typology breaking down intimate, acquaintance and stranger incidents.

Figure 4.4: Lifetime (since age of 16) and last year prevalence by sex

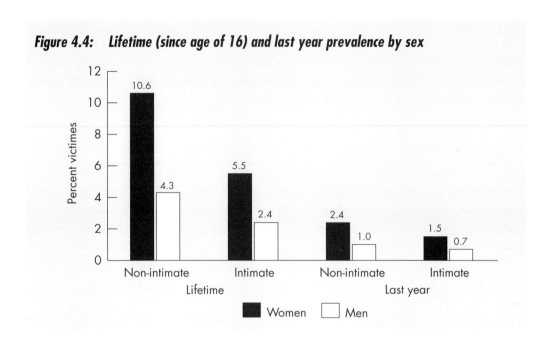

Tables A4.6 and A4.7 in Appendix A give the prevalence figures by age and sex.

Using this typology to re-examine the offender profile shows that intimate incidents were more likely to involve just one offender than non-intimate incidents (though this is not significant for female victims). Whether the incident involved an intimate or not, men were far more likely to be targeted by a group of offenders than women (Table A4.8).

In terms of the sex of offenders, as one would expect, the majority of intimate incidents involved an offender of the opposite sex, though this is less marked for men. Almost a third of intimate incidents against men involved male offenders (Table A4.9). The majority of non-intimate incidents, whether against women or men, were committed by men. Seventy-two per cent of male, non-intimate incidents were perpetrated by men, as were 88 per cent of female, non-intimate incidents.

Tjaden and Thoennes (1998) also found that the majority of stranger or acquaintance incidents against men involved male offenders. They hypothesised that some of these incidents could be because the victim was homosexual, with the offender being motivated either by homophobic attitudes or sexual attraction. Other incidents could relate to inter- or intra-group gang rivalries. The NVAW Survey did not collect information to enable these hypotheses to be tested.

The BCS does provide some insight into male on male incidents. The majority of such incidents were committed by strangers (42%), though five per cent were carried out by a current or former partner. The most common reason given for male on male incidents was that the offender wished to upset or annoy the victim, mentioned in 41 per cent of incidents. The desire to start or continue a relationship with the victim was only mentioned in 5 per cent of male/male incidents.

Table A4.10 in Appendix A examines the reasons given by victims by the stalking typology.

Chapter 5   Experiences of stalking

The BCS self-completion was specifically designed to capture a wide range of incidents that could potentially be considered as episodes of stalking. As discussed in Chapter 1, respondents were first asked if they had ever been the subject of persistent and unwanted attention. Those who had been were then asked details about the most recent episode that they had experienced. This and the following two chapters explore in detail the nature of the stalking incidents reported to the survey.

This chapter examines the duration of stalking episodes and the types and frequency of behaviours experienced. Chapter 6 discusses the impact of stalking incidents upon victims, while Chapter 7 considers the type of support and advice that victims seek.

Asking victims about their most recent incident is an accepted way of gathering details of a representative sample of incidents. However, as mentioned in Chapter 4, for those individuals who had experienced more than one episode of stalking since the age of 16 it is understandable if they reported details of their most serious episode, or most typical experience, rather than strictly the most recent. This could potentially bias any results presented here, if anything towards a more serious picture.

It should also be noted that in 21 per cent of stalking episodes more than one offender was involved. Where this was the case victims were only asked about the behaviour of the main offender.[34]

Length of persistent and unwanted attention

Victims were asked how long their most recent episode of stalking lasted. In about a third of cases the persistent and unwanted attention lasted less than a month, and in a further quarter (26%) between one and three months. However, for around one in five victims (19%) the persistent and unwanted attention lasted for a year or more. There were few differences between male and female victims (Figure 5.1).

---

34 In incidents where the victim was unable to identify one main offender they were instructed just to select any one of the offenders to talk about.

Figure 5.1:   Length of persistent and unwanted attention, by sex

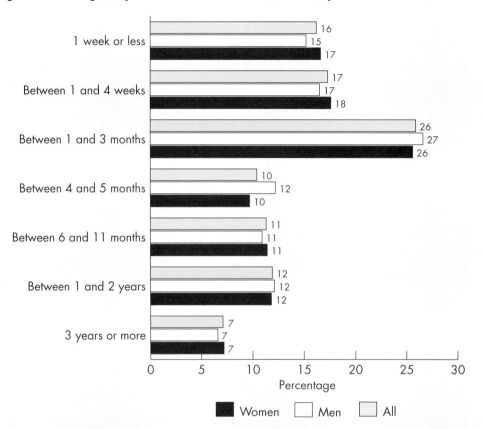

However, looking at the stalking typology (described in Chapter 4) reveals significant differences among women. Those who had a prior intimate relationship with their stalker experienced longer periods of stalking. More than a quarter (27%) of women who were stalked by an intimate had been stalked for at least a year, compared to 15 per cent of women stalked by a non–intimate (Table A5.1).

Nature of persistent and unwanted attention

Victims were asked a series of questions to establish what types of behaviour they had experienced. A total of 14 types of behaviour were asked about, ranging from unwanted gifts to sexual coercion (see Appendix F for the list of questions).

The most common experience was being forced into talking to the offender, with almost a half of all episodes (49%) involving this type of behaviour (Table A5.2). Other relatively common experiences, reported in a third or more of episodes, were:

- silent phone calls (45%)
- being physically intimidated (e.g. the perpetrator getting too close) (42%)
- being followed (39%)
- being touched or grabbed (34%)
- the offender waiting outside the victim's home (33%).

The least common experience was being forced into a sexual act, though this was reported in seven per cent of stalking episodes.

There were some differences between men and women (Figure 5.2). Among women, being forced into talking to the offender was the most common experience (52%), while among male victims silent phone calls were most common (44%). Overall, women were more likely to experience almost all of the stalking behaviours asked about. This was particularly so for obscene phone calls, being forced to talk to the offender, the offender refusing to take no for an answer, being followed and physical intimidation. Men were more likely to report that the offender had threatened to use or actually used force or violence.

Figure 5.2: Types of persistent and unwanted attention, by sex

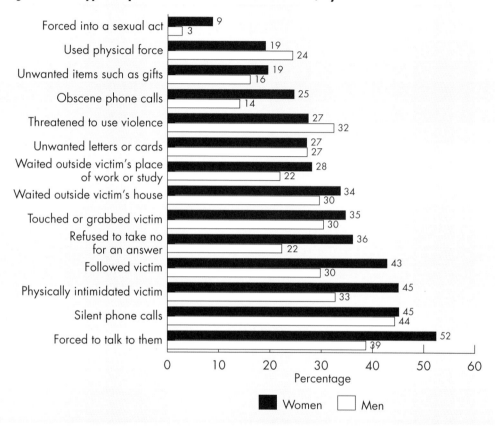

Further light can be shed on these findings by looking at the stalking typology. Overall, female victims who knew their offender intimately were the most likely to have experienced almost all types of persistent and unwanted attention listed in the survey (Table A5.3). The only exception to this was obscene phone calls, which were more likely to be experienced by women stalked by a non-intimate.[35]

Among men too, those who had known their offender intimately were more likely to have reported most of the types of persistent and unwanted attention. The exceptions to this were where the perpetrator had physically intimidated the victim, threatened to use violence or actually used physical force. This could be a reflection of the victim/offender gender breakdown. As we described in Chapter 4 the most likely gender relationship between the victim and perpetrator in a male non-intimate episode of stalking was a male offender stalking a male victim.

---

35 It is difficult to say what respondents understood by the term 'obscene phone calls'. It could have ranged from swearing to being sexually explicit and/or threatening – although the most likely outcome was that 'obscene phone calls' captured all of these. The 1982 and 1992 BCS included more detailed questions on obscene, threatening and other troublesome telephone calls to women (Buck et al., 1995).

Patterns of victimisation

The previous section discussed the prevalence of various stalking behaviours among those who had been subjected to persistent and unwanted attention. It is possible to take this one step further and examine the patterns of behaviour experienced within episodes of stalking. Admittedly, with a limited number of closed questions we can only examine patterns in a fairly rudimentary way. In-depth interviews would be required to explore in detail how stalking incidents progress, escalate and cease (see for example Coleman, 1997).

Number of behaviours experienced

Previous research has indicated that many stalking victims are subjected to a range of stalking behaviours (for example, Sheridan et al. (forthcoming)). The BCS findings confirm this. The vast majority (78%) of victims had experienced more than one of the 14 types of behaviour listed during their most recent episode. About a half of victims had been subjected to between two and five distinct types of behaviour and a further third to six or more (Figure 5.3). Seven per cent of victims of persistent and unwanted attention did not report experiencing any of the 14 types of behaviour. This is discussed further later in this chapter.

Figure 5.3: ***Number of different types of persistent and unwanted attention experienced by the victim***

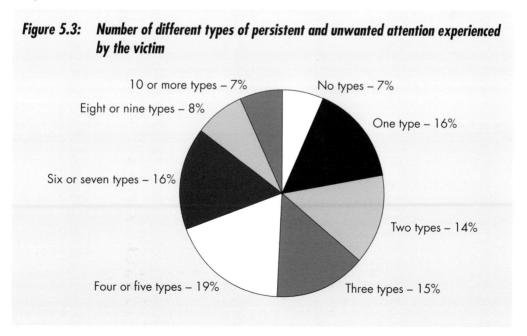

Overall, women tended to experience more types of behaviour than men. Thirty-three per cent of women reported experiencing six or more distinct types of behaviour, compared to 25 per cent of men (Table A5.4). Looking at the stalking typology, 60 per cent of women stalked by an intimate experienced six or more types of behaviour. The figure among women stalked by a non-intimate was 19 per cent (Table A5.5). Among men too, those stalked by an intimate were more likely to be subjected to six or more behaviours (34% compared to 20% for non-intimate incidents).

Some types of persistent and unwanted attention tend to occur in isolation, while others occur in combination with a range of behaviours. For example, episodes in which the victim received silent phone calls were least likely to involve other types of stalking behaviour. Episodes of stalking which involved the more serious types of behaviours, such as forcing the victim into a sexual act against their will, often also involved many other types of behaviour as well (Table A5.6).[36] However, we cannot establish from the survey the sequence of incidents and therefore to what extent types of behaviour escalate over time.

Frequency of behaviours

The BCS asked victims of persistent and unwanted attention how many times each distinct type of behaviour occurred. The full results are given in Table A5.7.

Within episodes of stalking, most of the types of persistent and unwanted attention were experienced on many occasions. Silent phone calls were most likely to occur on multiple occasions. Nine in ten of those who had experienced silent phone calls reported three or more occasions, with 43 per cent reporting more than ten incidents (Figure 5.4). The more serious behaviours tended to be least likely to occur on multiple occasions though the level of repeat incidents is still relatively high. For example, in 32 per cent of cases where physical force had been used, this had happened on three or more occasions, while in cases involving sexual coercion, 14 per cent of victims were forced into a sexual act on three or more occasions.

---

36 The relative seriousness of different types of persistent and unwanted attention will be revisited later in the chapter.

Figure 5.4: Percentage of victims that experienced each type of unwanted and persistent attention more than 10 times

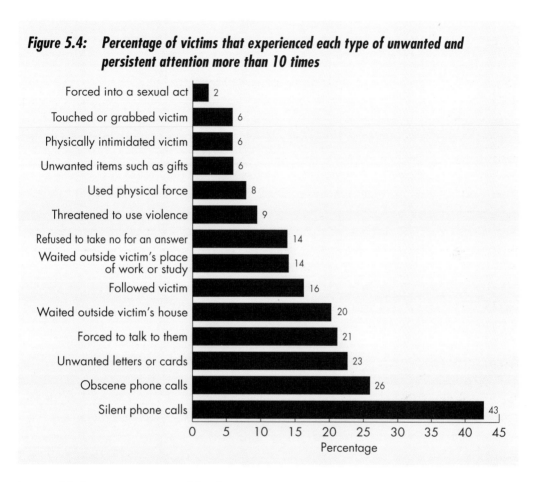

Types of behaviour not captured by the BCS

In seven per cent of episodes of persistent and unwanted attention (80 cases) the victim did not report any of the 14 types of stalking listed in the survey (Figure 5.3). Male non-intimate victims were most likely to recount this (Table A5.5). It is impossible from the BCS to ascertain the types of behaviours these respondents had characterised as persistent and unwanted attention.

However, the 14 types included in the BCS were by no means comprehensive. Sheridan et al. (forthcoming) gave their (female) respondents 42 intrusive behaviours, and asked them to select all those that they considered to be exemplars of stalking behaviour.[37] Using cluster analysis they found that for 25 of the 42 types of behaviour there was a high degree of

---

37 Respondents were asked to think of the behaviours being carried out exclusively by males toward a female victim.

consensus that these constituted stalking.[38] Some notable omissions from the BCS list include intercepting mail/deliveries, threatening behaviour towards the victim's family and/or friends and criminal damage/vandalism to the victim's property.

It should also be remembered that had the BCS stalking module been completed on paper, respondents would have been able to see the full list of questions and possibly 'fitted' their experiences into the most appropriate category. BCS CASI respondents could only see one question on the laptop screen at a time. So for instance, if a respondent had received repeated phone calls that were neither silent nor obscene but were persistent and unwanted they would answer no to both these questions, possibly presuming a question that fitted their experiences would be asked later. If the questionnaire had been on paper the respondent would have been able to see that only silent and obscene telephone calls were covered, and it is arguable they would have answered positively to at least one of these.

A typology of stalking behaviour

The BCS shows that most victims experienced more than one type of behaviour during the period of persistent and unwanted attention (Figure 5.3).

The exact pattern of stalking behaviour experienced will influence how victims react and the type of help or advice they require. It is neither feasible nor desirable to examine all possible stalking scenarios. However, when assessing the impact of an episode of stalking it is arguable that particular types of behaviour within the episode will have far more impact on the victim than others and will be more salient in the respondent's mind. A six-fold typology of victim experiences was developed which takes into account perceptions of the relative 'seriousness' of different episodes of stalking.

Appendix B describes in detail how the typology was developed. In essence, cluster analysis was used to identify which types of behaviour tended to occur together within episodes. The six resulting clusters were then ranked in terms of seriousness. Relative seriousness was assessed by examining responses to questions on fear of violence, whether the victim perceived the incident to be a crime and the emotional impact of the episode of stalking. It was necessary to develop a ranking mechanism because most victims (72%) experienced behaviours that cut across more than one of the clusters.

---

38 Defined in the study as "a series of actions directed at one individual by another which, taken as a whole, amount to unwanted persistent personal harassment".

Box 5.1 lists the six clusters identified in ascending order of seriousness with the types of behaviours included in each cluster and the number of stalking episodes allocated to each.

Box 5.1: Six-fold stalking typology

Cluster	Behaviours included	Number of episodes
Gifts and letters	Sending unwanted items: gifts, letters, cards etc Waiting outside place of work/study Refusing to take no for an answer	30
Silent phone calls	Silent phone calls	106
Followed	Following Waiting outside home Being forced into talking to the offender	235
Obscene phone calls	Obscene phone calls	115
Violence or threat of violence	Use of physical violence Touching or grabbing Threat of physical violence Physical intimidation	600
Sexual assault	Forcing victim into a sexual act	96

How the victims were assigned to groups within the stalking typology is best illustrated using examples. One example is when the victim had experienced three distinct types of behaviour during the episode of persistent and unwanted attention; the offender had made both silent and obscene phone calls and had used physical force. In this case the victim would be categorised as in the 'violence or threat of violence' group as this is defined as the most serious. However, if the victim had only experienced two of these behaviours; silent and obscene phone calls, the 'obscene phone calls' group would take precedence.

Half of all victims (50%) fall into the violence or threat of violence group of the six-fold typology, with a further fifth (20%) falling into the 'followed' group. This is true for both men and women (Figure 5.5). However, there are differences depending on the victim/offender relationship. Among male victims incidents involving a non-intimate are most likely to be categorised in the violence or threat of violence group (57%, as opposed to 45% for intimate incidents). For female victims intimate incidents are more likely to be in this group (59%, vs. 45% for non-intimate incidents) (Table A5.8). The relationship between the perpetrator and the victim highlights other significant differences. For example, 17 per cent of non-intimate episodes against female victims are classified as obscene phone calls, compared with just three per cent of intimate episodes.

Figure 5.5: Proportion of victims in each group of the six-fold typology

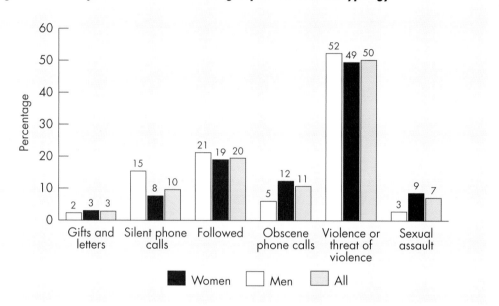

This typology will be used in the following chapters to examine how the impact of stalking episodes and the type of help sought varies according to the type of persistent and unwanted attention experienced.[39]

39 Throughout Chapters 6 and 7 the unweighted Ns for the 'gifts and letters' group were too small for reliable analysis.

Chapter 6   Impact upon the victim

This chapter explores the emotional impact of stalking, changes victims make in their lifestyle as a result of their experience and their fears of further victimisation. Finally, the chapter examines whether victims of persistent and unwanted attention are more concerned about crime generally than those who had not been a recent victim of any crime.

Emotional impact

Those who had been subject to persistent and unwanted attention were asked if the incidents had left them feeling annoyed/irritated or distressed/upset. Overall, 92 per cent of victims said they were annoyed or irritated (Figure 6.1). Seventy per cent were very annoyed or irritated with a further 21 per cent feeling fairly annoyed or irritated. Levels of distress or upset were lower, but still three-quarters had found the experience distressing or upsetting (50% very and 24% fairly). Women were more likely to be emotionally affected in these ways than men, particularly in terms of being distressed or upset – 57 per cent of women compared to 32 per cent of men saying they were very upset.

Figure 6.1:   *Emotional impact of persistent and unwanted attention, by sex of victim*

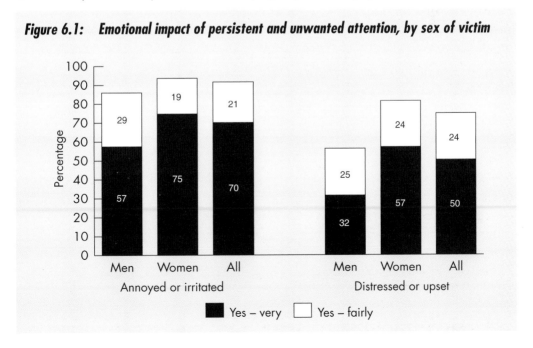

Among women levels of annoyance and distress were similar regardless of their relationship with the offender. However, among men those victimised by a non-intimate were most affected. Sixty-five per cent were very annoyed, with 35 per cent being very distressed. In incidents involving intimates the figures were 45 per cent and 26 per cent respectively (Table A6.1).

In terms of the stalking behaviour typology introduced in the previous chapter, those victims who had been sexually assaulted were most likely to be both very annoyed and distressed (85% and 79% respectively) (Table A6.2). Victims who had either experienced violence (or threat of violence) or obscene phone calls also had relatively high levels of annoyance and distress.

Other studies have also found that stalking can have profound effects. In a clinical sample of 100 victims, Pathé and Mullen (1997) found that 83 per cent experienced increased levels of anxiety, 55 per cent intrusive recollections and flashbacks, and 24 per cent had considered suicide. Nightmares, appetite disturbances and depression were also "commonly reported". To date there have been no long-term studies of the effects of stalking. There is, though, some evidence linking stalking victims with Post Traumatic Stress Disorder (PTSD). Pathé and Mullen (1997) found 37 per cent of their sample exhibited criteria for diagnosis of PTSD.

Impact on lifestyle

The effects of stalking on victims' general lives can also be limiting. Victims were asked whether their experience resulted in them changing their lifestyle or behaviour in the following ways:

- avoiding certain places or people
- going out less often
- taking extra security measures.

Overall, 71 per cent of those who had been the subject of persistent and unwanted attention said they had changed their behaviour in at least one of these ways (Figure 6.2). Fifty-nine per cent had avoided certain places or people, 42 per cent started taking additional personal security measures[40] and 35 per cent went out less than they had previously. On all three measures women were more likely to have changed their lifestyle than men. Overall, 76 per cent of women and 59 per cent of men reported that they had changed their behaviour in at least one of the three ways.

---

40 Although, respondents were not asked what types of additional security measures they had taken this could include carrying a personal alarm, increasing household security, driving or using public transport rather than walking or going out accompanied by another person.

Figure 6.2: Impact on the lifestyle of the victim, by sex

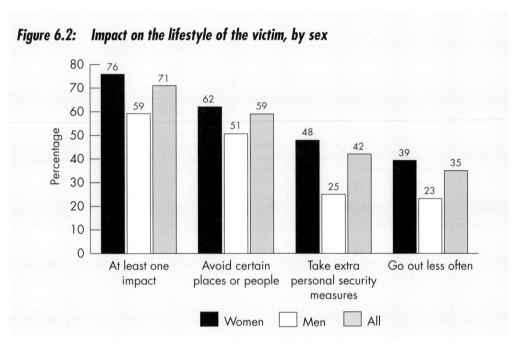

Regardless of whether they had an intimate relationship with the perpetrator or not, around three-quarters of female victims and six in ten male victims reported that their lifestyle had changed in at least one way. There were, though, some differences when looking at the various types of reaction.

Women stalked by an intimate were significantly more likely to avoid certain places or people and go out less often than women stalked by a non-intimate (Table A6.3). Conversely the only significant difference between male intimate and non-intimate episodes of stalking was that those who did not know their perpetrator well were more likely to take extra personal security measures (33% compared with 12%). This is perhaps a reflection of the fact that episodes of male non-intimate stalking are more likely to involve physical violence.[41]

Looking at the behaviour typology, those victims who had experienced sexual assault were the most likely to have changed their lifestyles, followed by those who experienced some form of physical intimidation, violence or the threat of violence (Table A6.4).

The effects covered by the BCS are by no means comprehensive. Other studies have shown a wide range of effects. For example, Tjaden and Thoennes (1998) found that 26 per cent of their victims said they took time off work, and seven per cent never returned to work as a result of their victimisation.

---

41 See Chapter 5 for further information.

Fears of further victimisation

Victims of persistent and unwanted attention were not only asked about what types of behaviour they had experienced but also whether they had feared the perpetrator would use violence, either against themselves or anyone they knew, or commit a sexual offence. The question on fearing violence against themselves was not asked of those victims who had experienced violence. Similarly the question on fearing a sexual attack was not asked of those who had actually been forced into a sexual act.[42]

Almost a third (31%) of victims were very or fairly afraid that violence would be used against them. A similar proportion (27%) were afraid violence would be used against a friend, relative or someone else they knew. Victims were less likely to fear a sexual offence, though 17 per cent did so (Figure 6.3). Women were far more fearful than men in relation to sexual assaults and somewhat more fearful of violence being used against themselves. Men were more concerned about violence being directed at someone they knew.

Figure 6.3: Fear of further victimisation, by sex

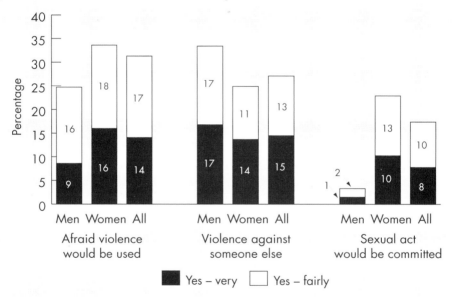

Women stalked by a non-intimate were far more worried about being sexually assaulted than those stalked by an intimate. They were also slightly more worried about the use of violence against themselves. Among men, those stalked by a non-intimate were more worried about violence against both themselves and people they knew.

42 Consequently it is not possible to look at these results by the behaviour typology.

Comparing victims' and non-victims' concerns

Multivariate analysis of the 1994 BCS provided strong evidence of the link between fear of crime and experience of crime (Hough, 1995). Tjaden and Thoennes (1998) found that victims of stalking were 'significantly' more likely than non-victims to be very concerned about their own personal safety. The 1998 BCS supports this.

The BCS asked all respondents how worried they were about various crimes and also how safe they felt in their own home and walking alone after dark. Table 6.1 examines the views of stalking victims with those who had not been a victim of any crime in the last year. The results show that women who had been a victim of stalking in the last year were more likely to be very worried about mugging/robbery and rape than those who had not been a victim of stalking or any BCS crime. They were also significantly more likely to feel very unsafe when alone after dark either at home or walking.

Table 6.1: Victims and non-victims[3] concerns about crime

	Not victim of stalking or BCS crime[3]	Victim of stalking in the last year	Statistically significant?[4]
Women[5]			
Percentage feeling very unsafe when...			
Walking alone after dark	12	20	Yes
Alone in own home after dark	2	5	Yes
Percentage very worried about...			
Mugging and robbery	22	30	Yes
Rape	32	42	Yes
Physical attack by a stranger	28	34	No

Notes:
1. Source: 1998 British Crime Survey.
2. Definition of stalking: persistent and unwanted attention (excluding incidents in which the victim and perpetrator were living with each other throughout the period over which the incidents occurred).
3. Those respondents aged 16 to 59 who had not been a victim of a BCS crime during the recall period (typically January 1997 to March 1998) and had not been a victim of stalking in the last year.
4. At the 10 per cent (two tail) level.
5. Unweighted Ns for female non-victims was around 2,840, for victims the figure was 230. Unweighted Ns for male victims were too small for reliable analysis.

This analysis however has some caveats. Firstly, the analysis compares those who have been a victim of stalking in the last year to those who have not experienced any BCS crime in the last year. The analysis does not compare the attitudes of stalking victims to victims of other types of crime. Moreover, being a victim can influence an individual's perceptions and fears for many years. Those classified as not BCS crime victims may have been victimised before the reference period. Secondly, although the results are statistically significant this does not necessarily indicate a causal relationship between victimisation and levels of fear.

Chapter 7   Seeking help

This chapter considers the extent to which victims of stalking sought help from the police and other sources, and how satisfied they were with the way the police handled the matter. First though, it examines victims' perceptions as to whether what happened to them constituted a crime.

Was it a crime?

Those who had experienced persistent and unwanted attention were asked whether they thought what had happened to them was a crime, wrong but not a crime or just something that happens. One-third of victims (33%) considered what had happened to be a crime and a further 37 per cent considered it to be 'wrong but not a crime'. Men and women were almost equally likely to consider their experience to be a crime. However, men tended to be less likely than women to consider their experience as 'wrong but not a crime' and more likely to consider it to be 'just something that happens' (Figure 7.1).

Figure 7.1: **Was the incident a crime, by sex**

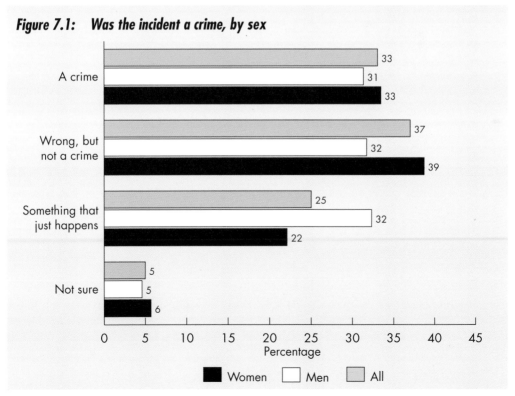

The victim/offender relationship does not appear to influence female victims' views, though among men those who did not have an intimate relationship with their offender were more than twice as likely to consider what had happened to them to be a crime (39% vs. 18%, Table A7.1). Needless to say, the type of behaviours experienced by the victim affected their assessment considerably, with 65 per cent of victims who had been sexually assaulted classifying their experience as a crime compared with only 12 per cent of those who had been followed (Table A7.2).

Asking victims whether they felt what happened was a crime is a relatively crude way of assessing whether the episode actually does fall within the scope of the criminal justice system. Victims may not always be correct for various reasons. Harris (2000) states that "most complainants were not aware of the Protection from Harassment Act...most do not realise that the behaviour to which they were subjected might now be an offence". Furthermore, responses to the question will not necessarily signify the degree of harm of distress caused to the victim. Something that 'just happens' may still have been frightening (Percy and Mayhew, 1997).

Contact with the police

Victims who considered their experience to be a crime were, not surprisingly, most likely to have reported the incident to the police – 56 per cent did so.[43] This compares to 24 per cent who classified their episode of persistent and unwanted attention as 'wrong but not a crime', and just 18 per cent who said it was 'something that just happens' (Table A7.3). It should be remembered that a victim's assessment of whether their experience was a crime is a retrospective one made at the time of interview. It could be that those who did not consider their incident to be a crime reported the incident to the police because at the time they did believe it to be a crime, or perhaps they feared the stalking could escalate. Conversely, victims who thought the episode was not a crime may have still considered it to be a matter for the police.

Proportion of victims reporting to the police

Overall, 33 per cent of victims said the police were aware of their most recent episode of persistent and unwanted attention (Figure 7.2). There were few differences in reporting to the police between male and female victims. Likewise, among women levels of reporting were

---

43 This could have been either the victim reporting the episode themselves, someone else reporting the incident, or the police coming to know about the incident in some other way.

similar regardless of their relationship with the offender. However, the police were significantly more likely to be aware of incidents against men where they had been victimised by a non-intimate. Thirty-eight per cent of men who were stalked by a non-intimate said the police knew. In incidents involving intimates the figure was 23 per cent (Table A7.4).

Figure 7.2: *Whether the police came to know about the episode of persistent and unwanted attention, by sex*

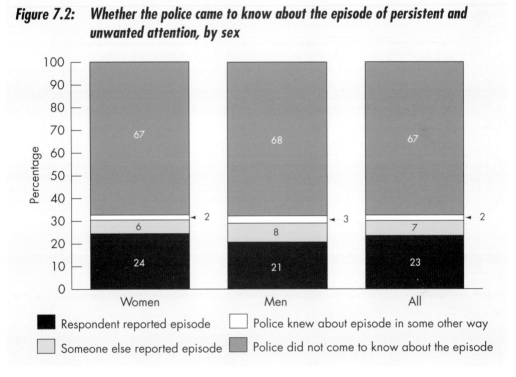

In terms of the stalking behaviour typology introduced in Chapter 5, the police were most likely to know about incidents involving obscene phone calls (43%). Victims who had either experienced violence (or threat of violence) or sexual assault were also more likely to involve the police, though this only happened in a third of incidents (Table A7.5).

Number of victims reporting to the police

Using the methodology outlined in Chapter 2 it is possible to estimate the number of victims of persistent and unwanted attention the police were aware of during the last year.[44] The 1998 BCS estimates that the police were aware of 294,000 adults aged 16 to 59 in England and Wales who had experienced persistent and unwanted attention in the last year (Table 7.1).[45,46]

This is the 'best' estimate of the number of victims. Because they are based on a sample of the population, they are subject to sampling error and may differ to the true number of victims in the population. Table 7.1 shows the best estimates and the range within which there is 95 per cent chance that the true figures lie. For example, there is 95 per cent chance that the true number of victims the police came to know about in the last year lies between 196,000 and 391,000. There is further discussion of sampling error in Appendix E.

Table 7.1: Number of victims who the police came to know about

	Best estimate (thousands)	Lowest estimate (thousands)	Highest estimate (thousands)
Last year estimate	294	196	391
Women	207	151	264
Men	86	45	127

Notes:
1. Source: 1998 British Crime Survey and ONS mid 1998 population estimates.
2. The estimates are subject to sampling error. The lowest and highest estimates are based on 95 per cent confidence intervals and assume a design effect of 1.2.

Satisfaction with the police

All victims who said the police came to know about their most recent episode of persistent and unwanted attention were asked whether they were satisfied with the way the police handled the matter. Overall, 61% of victims said they were satisfied, with 29% stating they were 'very satisfied' (Figure 7.3). However, a substantial minority were dissatisfied (35%).

---

44 It should be noted that the last year prevalence question asked about experience over the 12 months prior to the interview. Because interviews took place between January and June 1998 the recall period will vary depending on the date of interview. For example, for interviews which took place in March 1998, the respondent will be asked whether any of the persistent and unwanted attention took place since March 1997.

45 Estimates of the number of victims the police were aware of are derived by multiplying prevalence rates by the total number of adults aged 16 to 59 in England and Wales in 1998.

46 It is not known how many incidents reported to the police are recorded by them. This is because incidents could be recorded under many different offence categories.

Women tended to be more dissatisfied than men (although this was not statistically significant).[47]

Figure 7.3: Victims' satisfaction with the police, by sex

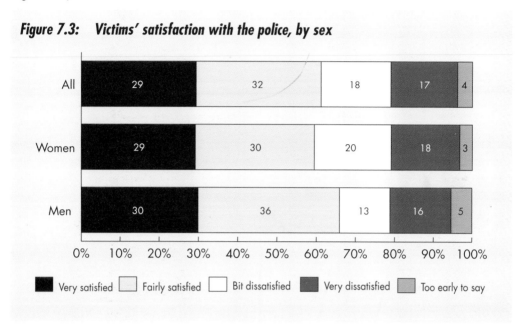

Telling others

In addition to the police, there are many other sources of support and advice victims can potentially turn to. The BCS asked all victims whether they had told anyone about the incident. Four-fifths of victims (82%) stated they had told someone (including the police). These respondents were then asked whether they had told each of the following three groups; their partner, boyfriend or girlfriend (55% of all victims), a friend, relative or neighbour (72%) and finally a doctor, social worker or carer (8%) (Figure 7.4).

Women were significantly more likely to confide in someone than men (85% vs. 73%). Overall, the offender/victim relationship did not influence a victim's propensity to tell someone about the incident. Having said that, who they told differed greatly. Not surprisingly, victims who had had an intimate relationship with the offender at some point were far less likely to tell their partner, boyfriend or girlfriend about their experience – potentially they were the perpetrator (Table A7.6).

---

47 Unweighted numbers were not sufficient to look at satisfaction with the police by either of the stalking typologies.

Figure 7.4:   Who the victim told about the persistent and unwanted attention, by sex

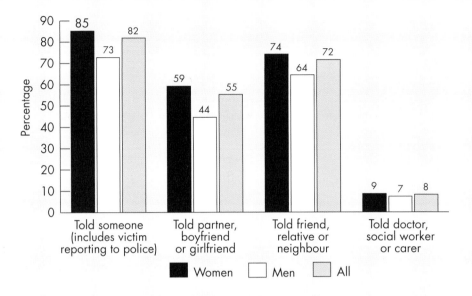

Looking at the behaviour typology, as with reporting to the police those victims who had experienced obscene phone calls were most likely to confide in someone (92%). Those least likely to report the incident to anyone were victims of sexual assault, with only 71% stating they had told someone (Table A7.7).

Chapter 8   Discussion

The findings in this report are based on an innovative self-completion questionnaire included in the 1998 British Crime Survey (BCS) which was designed to capture a wide range of experiences that could potentially be regarded as incidents of stalking. This concluding chapter highlights findings of relevance in developing policy for victims of stalking.

Extent of the problem

This BCS self-completion module provides the first reliable, national level picture of the extent of stalking in England and Wales. According to the BCS, 2.9% of all adults aged 16 to 59 were subjected to persistent and unwanted attention in the last year. This equates to about 900,000 victims (610,000 women and 270,000 men). These estimates are based on a relatively broad definition of stalking – 'persistent and unwanted attention' and Chapter 5 discusses in detail the types of experience captured.

The Protection from Harassment Act (1997) does not tightly define what would constitute harassment although it does state that it can include alarming the person or causing them distress. The Act created two offences: the summary offence of causing harassment or distress and the triable-either-way offence of putting people in fear of violence. Restricting the definition of stalking to incidents of persistent and unwanted attention which caused the victim upset or distress, the BCS estimates there were 770,000 victims in the last year. Restricting the definition to those episodes which involved violence or the threat of violence or in which the victim was fearful of violence results in an estimate of 550,000 victims.

Contact with the police

The BCS estimates that only a third of stalking incidents became known to the police, and even when incidents were considered by victims to be crimes only just over a half were reported. Furthermore, around a third of those who said they did report were dissatisfied with the police response. The BCS does not provide information about the source of victim dissatisfaction. Harris (2000), however, reported that some victims found difficulties when the police officer they had been dealing with was off duty and also felt they required more support to help them through the court process.

Since this research was conducted a new guidance document has been released for police officers dealing with cases of harassment of stalking.[48] The guidance also provides advice to victims. The launch of this document may well encourage the reporting of incidents to the police and improve the way in which the police deal with such incidents.

It may also be that Victim Support and Witness Service can play a bigger role in providing support and advice to victims of stalking and harassment. At present it is not mandatory for victims of harassment cases to be referred to Victim Support, though it should be said that the Victim Supportline introduced in February 1998 has made it easier for victims to contact Victim Support directly themselves. The Witness Service currently is only available in selected magistrates' courts, though by 2003 there will be a service provided in all courts.

Who are the victims?

Identifying those most at risk is useful in informing targeted support and intervention strategies. Women are far more at risk of persistent and unwanted attention than men. Women most at risk are:

- aged between 16 and 24
- single
- students
- living in privately rented accommodation
- living in a flat or a maisonette
- living in low income households (less than £15,000 per annum).

While women are more at risk, the experiences of men should not be ignored. The experiences of male victims seem to be rather different to those of female victims. Incidents against male victims were more likely to have involved more than one offender and more likely to involve someone previously known to the victim. Incidents against men were also more likely to involve the threat or actual use of violence. This said, women were more likely to experience a range of behaviours, including a sexual offence, and more likely to be distressed by their experience.

---

48 The guidance is 'Stalking and other forms of harassment; An investigator's guide' (Brown. 2000).

Who are the offenders?

Stalking incidents are stereotypically seen as being perpetrated by obsessive or psychotic strangers. However, almost two-thirds of stalking incidents measured involved a perpetrator who was previously known to the victim in some way. Around a third of incidents were committed by someone who was in an intimate relationship with the victim at the start of the episode of persistent and unwanted attention, or who was a former intimate. A further third were committed by an acquaintance of the victim. Only a third of incidents were committed by someone the victim did not know in any way prior to the incident.

The nature of stalking episodes

The BCS has shown that victims of persistent and unwanted attention experience a myriad of different types of behaviour. More importantly, a relatively high proportion of incidents involved what would be regarded as serious violent or sexual offences. Policy relating to stalking needs to take into account the variety and severity of experiences.

Furthermore, there appears to be some overlap between stalking, domestic and sexual violence. In 29 per cent of stalking incidents the perpetrator was a partner or former partner of the victim and in over four in ten of these incidents violence or the threat of violence had been used. Seven per cent of all stalking incidents involved some form of sexual assault. The inter linkage between these various types of interpersonal violence is an area for future research, and should be considered in any future policy developments.

Table A2.1: Lifetime (since age of sixteen) prevalence, by age and sex

Percent victims	Women	Men	All
Age			
16-19	22.6	8.9	15.7
20-24	19.2	13.3	16.9
25-29	19.0	8.0	14.1
30-34	16.9	6.4	12.2
35-39	15.5	5.4	10.8
40-44	16.5	7.4	12.3
45-49	14.0	5.0	9.7
50-54	13.0	5.5	9.4
55-59	10.2	4.0	7.1
All	16.1	6.8	11.8

Notes:
1. Source: 1998 British Crime Survey.
2. Definition of stalking: persistent and unwanted attention (excluding incidents in which the victim and perpetrator were living with each other throughout the period over which the incidents occurred).
3. All figures based on categories with 200 or more cases in the base.

Table A2.2:   Last year prevalence, by age and sex

Percent victims	Women	Men	All
Age			
16-19	16.8	3.1	9.9
20-24	7.8	4.6	6.5
25-29	5.3	2.0	3.8
30-34	3.2	1.5	2.5
35-39	2.4	1.1	1.8
40-44	1.9	1.4	1.6
45-49	1.9	1.0	1.4
50-54	1.0	1.5	1.3
55-59	1.4	1.1	1.2
All	4.0	1.7	2.9

Notes:
1. Source: 1998 British Crime Survey.
2. Definition of stalking: persistent and unwanted attention (excluding incidents in which the victim and perpetrator were living with each other throughout the period over which the incidents occurred).
3. All figures based on categories with 200 or more cases in the base.

Table A2.3:   Number of victims in England and Wales of incidents of persistent and unwanted attention (a) causing upset or distress and (b) involving violence, threat or fear of violence

	Best estimate (millions)	Lowest estimate (millions)	Highest estimate (millions)
Incidents causing upset or distress	0.77	0.61	0.92
Women	0.57	0.48	0.66
Men	0.20	0.14	0.26
Violence, threat of or fear of violence	0.55	0.42	0.68
Women	0.41	0.33	0.49
Men	0.14	0.09	0.20

Notes:
1. Source: 1998 British Crime Survey and ONS mid 1998 population estimates.
2. The estimates are subject to sampling error. The lowest and highest estimates are based on 95% confidence intervals and assume a design effect of 1.2.

Table A3.1:   Last year prevalence – risk factors

Percent victims	Women	Men	All
Age			
16 to 19	16.8	3.1	9.9
20 to 24	7.8	4.6	6.5
25 to 29	5.3	2.0	3.8
30 to 34	3.2	1.5	2.5
35 to 39	2.4	1.1	1.8
40 to 44	1.9	1.4	1.6
45 to 49	1.9	1.0	1.4
50 to 54	1.0	1.5	1.3
55 to 59	1.4	1.1	1.2
Marital status			
Married	1.4	1.1	1.2
Cohabiting	4.6	1.0	3.0
Single	9.8	3.7	6.7
Divorced	5.8	1.4	4.2
Separated	6.7	1.9	5.1
Widowed	2.1	-	1.6
Employment status			
Employed	3.6	1.7	2.6
Unemployed	7.1	2.1	4.0
Student	12.4	3.0	8.0
At home	2.8	-	2.7
Retired	0.8	-	0.5
Education level			
Degree or equivalent	3.7	1.8	2.8
A-level or equivalent	5.8	2.0	3.8
GCSE or equivalent	4.8	1.8	3.5
No qualifications	2.1	1.1	1.7
Household income			
Less than £15,000	5.3	3.2	4.5
£15,000 or more	3.1	1.2	2.2
Tenure type			
Owner occupier	2.7	1.4	2.1
Council or Housing Association	5.2	3.0	4.3
Private renter	7.4	2.0	4.8
Accommodation type			
Detached house	2.6	1.2	1.9
Semi-detached house	4.3	1.2	2.9
Terraced house	3.6	2.4	3.1
Flat/maisonette	6.6	2.8	4.8
Area			
Inner city or urban	4.1	2.1	3.2
Rural	3.4	0.7	2.1

Notes:
1.   Source: 1998 British Crime Survey.
2.   Definition of stalking: persistent and unwanted attention (excluding incidents in which the victim and perpetrator were living with each other throughout the period over which the incidents occurred).
3.   Bold indicates significantly higher (10% level) than the national average (for men and women significantly above the national average for men and women). - indicates no respondents in category were victims.
4.   All figures based on categories with 100 or more cases in the base, except widowed males; males at home and retired males and females.

Table A3.2 Last year prevalence, by Government Office Region

Percent victims	Women	Men	All
Region			
North East	3.1	1.7	2.5
North West	4.4	1.2	2.9
Merseyside	1.5	1.3	1.4
Yorkshire and Humberside	5.0	1.2	3.2
East Midlands	3.6	4.2	3.9
West Midlands	3.4	2.0	2.8
South West	5.0	1.8	3.5
Eastern	4.8	0.9	3.0
London	4.0	1.8	3.0
South East	3.7	1.7	2.7
Wales	2.2	1.2	1.7
All	4.0	1.7	2.9

Notes:
1. Source: 1998 British Crime Survey.
2. Definition of stalking: persistent and unwanted attention (excluding incidents in which the victim and perpetrator were living with each other throughout the period over which the incidents occurred).
3. Bold indicates the result is significantly higher (10% level) than the national average (for men and women significantly above the national average for men and women).
4. All figures based on categories with 100 or more cases in the base.

Table A4.1: Age and sex of offenders

	Women	Men	All
Offender was:	%	%	%
Male	90	57	81
Under 16	1	5	2
16 to 19	13	18	14
20 to 39	60	26	51
40 to 59	15	7	13
60 or older	1	1	1
Female	10	43	19
Under 16	1	2	1
16 to 19	2	11	4
20 to 39	5	24	10
40 to 59	2	6	3
60 or older	1	<1	1
Unweighted N	*899*	*294*	*1,193*
Offender was:	%	%	%
Under 16	2	7	4
16 to 19	14	29	18
20 to 39	64	49	60
40 to 59	17	13	16
60 or older	2	1	2
Unweighted N	*925*	*303*	*1,228*

Notes:
1. Source: 1998 British Crime Survey.
2. Definition of stalking: persistent and unwanted attention (excluding incidents in which the victim and perpetrator were living with each other throughout the period over which the incidents occurred).
3. <1 indicates less than 0.5%.

Table A4.2: Offender's relationship to the victim[3]

Offender was:	Women	Men	All
	%	%	%
Intimate	30	27	29
Spouse/partner	4	2	3
Ex-spouse/partner	5	5	5
Boyfriend/girlfriend	7	5	6
Ex boyfriend/girlfriend	7	8	7
Date	8	7	8
Relative/household member/close friend	4	8	6
Parent (including step and in-laws)	<1	1	<1
Child (including step and in-laws)	<1	1	1
Other relative	1	1	1
Other household member	<1	<1	<1
Close friend	2	5	3
Acquaintance	30	36	32
Employer/manager	1	1	1
Work colleague	6	5	6
Client/member of public contacted through work	2	2	2
Casual acquaintance	8	10	9
Other known	13	18	14
Stranger	35	28	34
Unweighted N	944	307	1,251

Notes:
1. Source: 1998 British Crime Survey.
2. Definition of stalking: persistent and unwanted attention (excluding incidents in which the victim and perpetrator were living with each other throughout the period over which the incidents occurred).
3. Relationship at the beginning of the episode of persistent and unwanted attention.
4. <1 indicates less than 0.5%.

Table A4.3: How well the offender known[3]

	Women	Men	All
Offender known:	%	%	%
Well	41	38	40
Casually	45	48	46
By sight	13	14	13
Unweighted N	*581*	*209*	*790*

Notes:
1. Source: 1998 British Crime Survey.
2. Definition of stalking: persistent and unwanted attention (excluding incidents in which the victim and perpetrator were living with each other throughout the period over which the incidents occurred).
3. Relationship at the beginning of the episode of persistent and unwanted attention. Episodes in which perpetrator was spouse/ex-spouse or stranger are excluded.

Table A4.4: Last year and lifetime (since age of sixteen) prevalence – intimate, acquaintance and stranger – by sex

Percent victims	Women	Men	All
Lifetime			
Intimate	5.5	2.4	4.1
Acquaintance	4.9	2.4	3.7
Stranger	5.7	1.9	3.9
Unweighted N	*5,458*	*4,369*	*9,827*
Last year			
Intimate	1.5	0.7	1.1
Acquaintance	1.2	0.5	0.9
Stranger	1.2	0.5	0.9
Unweighted N	*5,460*	*4,370*	*9,830*

Notes:
1. Source: 1998 British Crime Survey.
2. Definition of stalking: persistent and unwanted attention (excluding incidents in which the victim and perpetrator were living with each other throughout the period over which the incidents occurred).
3. Relationship at the beginning of the episode of persistent and unwanted attention. Intimate includes current and former spouse, partner, boy/girlfriend or date and relatives, close friends and other household members. Acquaintance includes all other people known to the victim either casually or just by sight. Stranger includes those people not known to the victim.

Table A4.5: Offender's relationship to the victim[3], by victim typology

Offender was:	Intimate incidents		
	Women	Men	All
	%	%	%
Intimate	87	77	84
Spouse/partner	10	6	9
Ex-spouse/partner	15	14	14
Boyfriend/girlfriend	19	13	17
Ex boyfriend/girlfriend	20	23	21
Date	22	21	22
Relative/household			
member/close friend	13	23	16
Parent (including step and in-laws)	1	1	1
Child (including step and in-laws)	1	4	2
Other relative	4	2	3
Other household member	1	1	1
Close friend	6	15	9
Unweighted N	*344*	*110*	*454*

	Non-intimate incidents		
	Women	Men	All
	%	%	%
Acquaintance	46	56	49
Employer/manager	2	1	2
Work colleague	9	7	9
Client/member of public			
contacted through work	3	4	3
Casual acquaintance	13	15	13
Other known	20	29	22
Stranger	54	44	51
Unweighted N	*600*	*197*	*797*

Notes:
1. Source: 1998 British Crime Survey.
2. Definition of stalking: persistent and unwanted attention (excluding incidents in which the victim and perpetrator were living with each other throughout the period over which the incidents occurred).
3. Relationship at the beginning of the episode of persistent and unwanted attention.

Table A4.6: Lifetime (since the age of sixteen) prevalence – intimate and non-intimate – by sex and age

Percent victims	Women		Men		All	
	Intimate	Non intimate	Intimate	Non intimate	Intimate	Non intimate
16-19	8.3	14.4	4.1	4.7	6.2	9.5
20-24	8.2	10.9	6.2	7.1	7.4	9.4
25-29	6.7	12.3	3.5	4.5	5.3	8.8
30-34	5.5	11.3	2.3	4.1	4.1	8.1
35-39	5.6	9.8	2.3	3.0	4.1	6.6
40-44	5.0	11.4	1.8	5.6	3.5	8.7
45-49	4.4	9.6	1.5	3.3	3.0	6.6
50-54	3.9	8.9	1.3	4.2	2.7	6.6
55-59	2.5	7.2	0.5	3.4	1.5	5.3
All	5.5	10.6	2.4	4.3	4.1	7.7

Notes:
1. Source: 1998 British Crime Survey.
2. Definition of stalking: persistent and unwanted attention (excluding incidents in which the victim and perpetrator were living with each other throughout the period over which the incidents occurred).
3. All figures based on categories with 200 or more cases in the base.

Table A4.7: Last year prevalence – intimate and non-intimate – by sex and age

Percent victims	Women		Men		All	
	Intimate	Non intimate	Intimate	Non intimate	Intimate	Non intimate
16-19	4.9	11.9	1.2	1.9	3.1	6.9
20-24	3.4	4.3	3.2	1.4	3.3	3.2
25-29	2.4	2.9	0.8	1.2	1.7	2.1
30-34	1.0	2.1	0.7	0.8	0.9	1.5
35-39	0.8	1.5	0.5	0.5	0.7	1.0
40-44	0.9	0.8	0.3	1.1	0.6	0.9
45-49	0.6	1.3	-	1.0	0.3	1.1
50-54	0.5	0.4	*	1.5	0.3	0.9
55-59	0.5	0.9	0.5	0.4	0.5	0.7
All	1.5	2.4	0.7	1.0	1.1	1.8

Notes:
1. Source: 1998 British Crime Survey.
2. Definition of stalking: persistent and unwanted attention (excluding incidents in which the victim and perpetrator were living with each other throughout the period over which the incidents occurred).
3. – indicates no respondents in this category were victims. * indicates a risk of less than 0.05%.
4. All figures based on categories with 200 or more cases in the base.

Table A4.8: Number of offenders, by victim typology

	Women		Men		All	
	Intimate	Non intimate	Intimate	Non intimate	Intimate	Non intimate
Number of offenders:	%	%	%	%	%	%
One	87	83	75	60	84	77
Two	8	8	12	16	9	10
Three	3	4	1	5	2	4
Four or more	2	6	12	18	5	9
Unweighted N	344	568	107	181	441	749

Notes:
1. Source: 1998 British Crime Survey.
2. Definition of stalking: persistent and unwanted attention (excluding incidents in which the victim and perpetrator were living with each other throughout the period over which the incidents occurred).

Table A4.9: Age and sex of offenders, by victim typology

	Women		Men		All	
	Intimate	Non intimate	Intimate	Non intimate	Intimate	Non intimate
	%	%	%	%	%	%
Male	94	88	30	72	76	84
Under 16	1	1	1	8	1	3
16 to 19	15	11	11	22	14	14
20 to 39	64	57	16	32	51	51
40 to 59	13	17	3	10	10	15
60 or older	1	2	-	1	<1	1
Female	6	12	70	28	24	16
Under 16	-	1	3	1	1	1
16 to 19	2	2	22	5	7	3
20 to 39	4	6	40	14	14	8
40 to 59	1	3	5	6	2	4
60 or older	-	1	-	1	-	1
Unweighted N	337	562	107	187	444	749
	%	%	%	%	%	%
All						
Under 16	2	3	4	9	3	4
16 to 19	17	13	34	26	22	17
20 to 39	67	63	54	46	63	59
40 to 59	14	19	8	16	12	18
60 or older	1	2	-	1	<1	2
Unweighted N	344	581	110	193	454	774

Notes:
1. Source: 1998 British Crime Survey.
2. Definition of stalking: persistent and unwanted attention (excluding incidents in which the victim and perpetrator were living with each other throughout the period over which the incidents occurred).
3. <1 indicates less than 0.5%. - indicates no respndents.

Table A4.10: *Reason for stalking by victim typology*

	Women		Men		All	
	Intimate	Non intimate	Intimate	Non intimate	Intimate	Non intimate
	%	%	%	%	%	%
To impress me	1	-	1	-	1	-
To upset/annoy me	5	17	13	34	7	21
To protect/guard me	3	<1	2	<1	3	<1
To start a relationship	11	31	13	17	12	28
To continue a relationship	38	-	23	-	34	-
Revenge now relationship over	10	-	15	-	11	-
Client demand services/goods	<1	1	-	2	<1	2
Employer/colleague demanding work	-	1	-	-	-	<1
To punish friend/relative	2	2	1	3	2	2
Other reason	20	19	21	27	20	21
Don't know	9	29	12	17	10	25
Unweighted N	*344*	*600*	*110*	*197*	*454*	*797*

Notes:
1. Source: 1998 British Crime Survey.
2. Definition of stalking: persistent and unwanted attention (excluding incidents in which the victim and perpetrator were living with each other throughout the period over which the incidents occurred).
3. <1 indicates less than 0.5. – indicates no respondents gave this answer.
4. Separate questions with different response options were asked depending on the victim/offender relationship (see Appendix F).

Table A5.1: Length of persistent and unwanted attention, by victim typology

	Women		Men		All	
	Intimate	Non intimate	Intimate	Non intimate	Intimate	Non intimate
	%	%	%	%	%	%
1 week or less	8	21	12	17	9	20
Between 1 and 4 weeks	14	20	21	14	16	18
Between 1 and 3 months	24	27	31	24	26	26
Between 4 and 5 months	14	7	12	12	13	9
Between 6 and 11 months	14	10	8	12	12	11
Between 1 and 2 years	14	11	9	14	13	11
3 years or more	13	4	6	7	11	5
Unweighted N	344	598	110	197	454	795

Notes:
1. Source: 1998 British Crime Survey.
2. Definition of stalking: persistent and unwanted attention (excluding incidents in which the victim and perpetrator were living with each other throughout the period over which the incidents occurred).

Table A5.2: Types of persistent and unwanted attention, by sex

Percentages	Women	Men	All
Unwanted letters or cards	27	27	27
Silent phone calls	45	44	45
Obscene phone calls	25	14	22
Unwanted items such as gifts	19	16	19
Forced to talk to them	52	39	49
Followed victim	43	30	39
Waited outside victim's house	34	30	33
Waited outside victim's place of work or study	28	22	26
Refused to take no for an answer	36	22	32
Physically intimidated victim	45	33	42
Touched or grabbed victim	35	30	34
Threatened to use violence[4]	27	32	29
Used physical force[4]	19	24	20
Forced victim into a sexual act against their will[4]	9	3	7

Notes:
1. Source: 1998 British Crime Survey.
2. Definition of stalking: persistent and unwanted attention (excluding incidents in which the victim and perpetrator were living with each other throughout the period over which the incidents occurred).
3. Don't knows are included in the base. A significant proportion of victims (more than 10% of all victims) said don't know to the following types of behaviour: followed victim (16%), waited outside victim's home (13%) and waited outside victim's place of work or study (12%).
4. Only those victims who had experienced any of the previous types of persistent and unwanted attention were asked these three questions.

Table A5.3: Types of persistent and unwanted attention, by victim typology

Percentage	Women		Men		All	
	Intimate	Non intimate	Intimate	Non intimate	Intimate	Non intimate
Unwanted letters or cards	44	18	43	19	44	18
Silent phone calls	54	41	49	41	52	41
Obscene phone calls	22	26	21	11	21	22
Unwanted items such as gifts	34	12	30	8	33	11
Forced to talk to them	69	44	55	30	65	41
Followed victim	52	39	34	28	47	36
Waited outside victim's house	55	23	36	26	50	24
Waited outside victim's place of work/study	40	22	22	22	35	22
Refused to take no for an answer	55	27	40	13	51	23
Physically intimidated victim	60	37	26	37	51	37
Touched or grabbed victim	54	25	34	29	49	26
Threatened to use violence[4]	44	19	20	40	37	24
Used physical force[4]	35	11	19	28	31	15
Forced into a sexual act[4]	16	5	4	2	13	4

Notes:
1. Source: 1998 British Crime Survey.
2. Definition of stalking: persistent and unwanted attention (excluding incidents in which the victim and perpetrator were living with each other throughout the period over which the incidents occurred).
3. Don't knows are included in the base. A significant proportion of victims (more than 10% of all victims) said don't know to the following types of behaviour: followed victim (16%), waited outside victim's home (13%) and waited outside victim's place of work or study (12%).
4. Only those victims who had experienced any of the previous types of persistent and unwanted attention were asked these three questions.

Table A5.4: *Number of different types of persistent and unwanted attention experienced by the victim, by sex*

	Women	Men	All
	%	%	%
No types	5	11	7
One type	15	18	16
Two types	15	11	14
Three types	15	14	15
Four or five types	18	20	19
Six or seven types	16	17	16
Eight or nine types	9	6	8
10 or more types	8	3	7
Unweighted N	952	310	1,262

Notes:
1. Source: 1998 British Crime Survey.
2. Definition of stalking: persistent and unwanted attention (excluding incidents in which the victim and perpetrator were living with each other throughout the period over which the incidents occurred).
3. Those respondents who said don't know to a type of behaviour or were not asked the question due to routing were re-coded as presuming the type of behaviour did not happen to them.

Table A5.5: Number of different types of persistent and unwanted attention experienced by the victim, by victim typology

	Women		Men		All	
	Intimate	Non intimate	Intimate	Non intimate	Intimate	Non intimate
	%	%	%	%	%	%
No types	4	5	8	13	5	7
One type	8	17	13	21	10	18
Two types	6	20	15	9	8	17
Three types	9	18	13	14	10	17
Four or five types	13	20	16	23	14	21
Six or seven types	24	11	19	16	23	12
Eight or nine types	17	5	10	3	15	4
10 or more types	19	3	5	2	15	2
Unweighted N	344	600	110	197	454	797

Notes:
1. Source: 1998 British Crime Survey.
2. Definition of stalking: persistent and unwanted attention (excluding incidents in which the victim and perpetrator were living with each other throughout the period over which the incidents occurred).
3. Those respondents who said don't know to a type of behaviour or were not asked the question due to routing were re-coded as presuming the type of behaviour did not happen to them.

Table A5.6: Number of different types of persistent and unwanted attention experienced by victims

Percentages	No other types	One other type	Two or three other types	Four or five other types	Six or more other types	Unweighted N
Type of persistent and unwanted attention						
Unwanted letters or cards	4	8	17	22	49	355
Silent phone calls	16	13	22	17	32	585
Obscene phone calls	7	16	27	15	34	268
Unwanted items such as gifts	1	2	13	24	60	255
Forced to talk to them	4	6	25	25	41	631
Followed victim	4	8	20	24	44	511
Waited outside victim's house	2	3	19	24	51	453
Waited outside victim's place of work or study	<1	7	19	22	51	335
Refused to take no for an answer	1	5	21	24	49	429
Physically intimidated victim	2	6	21	26	46	545
Touched or grabbed victim	1	5	17	23	54	439
Threatened to use violence[3]	NA[3]	6	20	26	48	365
Used physical force[3]	NA[3]	1	13	24	62	269
Forced victim into a sexual act against their will[3]	NA[3]	-	11	21	68	96

Notes:
1. Source: 1998 British Crime Survey.
2. Definition of stalking: persistent and unwanted attention (excluding incidents in which the victim and perpetrator were living with each other throughout the period over which the incidents occurred).
3. Only those victims who had experienced any of the previous types of persistent and unwanted attention were asked these three questions.
4. In each case the percentages refers to the number of other types of persistent and unwanted attention experienced by the victim.
5. <1 indicates less than 0.5%.
6. – indicates nil.

Table A5.7: Number of times each type of persistent and unwanted attention occurred

Percentages	Once	Twice	Three to 10 times	11 to 50 times	More than 50 times	*Unweighted N*
Unwanted letters or cards	9	16	53	18	5	*355*
Silent phone calls	2	8	47	31	12	*585*
Obscene phone calls	9	17	48	20	6	*268*
Unwanted items such as gifts	19	32	43	6	<1	*255*
Forced to talk to them	14	15	50	18	3	*631*
Followed victim	19	19	45	14	2	*511*
Waited outside victim's house	16	18	46	18	2	*451*
Waited outside victim's place of work or study	15	24	47	13	1	*334*
Refused to take no for an answer	18	22	46	14	<1	*428*
Physically intimidated victim	31	25	38	6	<1	*544*
Touched or grabbed victim	37	26	31	6	<1	*439*
Threatened to use violence[3]	33	25	32	8	2	*365*
Used physical force[3]	47	21	24	7	1	*269*
Forced victim into a sexual act against their will[3]	66	20	12	2	-	*96*

Notes:
1. Source: 1998 British Crime Survey.
2. Definition of stalking: persistent and unwanted attention (excluding incidents in which the victim and perpetrator were living with each other throughout the period over which the incidents occurred).
3. Only those victims who had experienced any of the previous types of persistent and unwanted attention were asked these three questions.
4. <1 indicates less than 0.5%.
5. – indicates nil.

Table A5.8:   Proportion of victims in each group of the six-fold behaviour typology

	Women		Men		All	
	Intimate	Non intimate	Intimate	Non intimate	Intimate	Non intimate
	%	%	%	%	%	%
Gifts and letters	3	3	4	1	4	2
Silent phone calls	4	9	11	17	6	11
Followed	16	21	26	19	18	20
Obscene phone calls	3	17	10	3	5	14
Violence or threat of violence	59	45	45	57	55	48
Sexual assault	15	5	4	2	12	4
Unweighted N	336	564	103	172	439	736

Notes:
1. Source: 1998 British Crime Survey.
2. Definition of stalking: persistent and unwanted attention (excluding incidents in which the victim and perpetrator were living with each other throughout the period over which the incidents occurred).
3. Those respondents who did not experience any of the 14 types of behaviour listed in the BCS are excluded from the base.

Table A6.1: Emotional impact of persistent and unwanted attention, by victim typology

	Women		Men		All	
	Intimate	Non intimate	Intimate	Non intimate	Intimate	Non intimate
Annoyed or irritated	%	%	%	%	%	%
Yes – very	79	73	45	65	70	71
Yes – fairly	16	21	38	24	22	21
Yes – a little	3	5	13	9	6	6
Not at all	2	1	4	3	3	2
Unweighted N	*344*	*600*	*110*	*197*	*454*	*797*
Distressed or upset	%	%	%	%	%	%
Yes – very	57	57	26	35	48	52
Yes – fairly	27	23	23	26	26	24
Yes – a little	12	16	25	23	15	17
Not at all	5	4	27	16	11	7
Unweighted N	*344*	*600*	*110*	*197*	*454*	*797*

Notes:
1. Source: 1998 British Crime Survey.
2. Definition of stalking: persistent and unwanted attention (excluding incidents in which the victim and perpetrator were living with each other throughout the period over which the incidents occurred).

Table A6.2: *Emotional impact of persistent and unwanted attention, by behaviour typology*

	Silent phone calls	Followed	Obscene phone calls	Violence or threat of violence	Sexual assault
Annoyed or irritated	%	%	%	%	%
Yes – very	62	56	76	78	85
Yes — fairly	25	31	18	18	14
Yes – a little	12	11	5	3	2
Not at all	1	2	1	1	-
Unweighted N	*106*	*235*	*115*	*600*	*96*
Distressed or upset	%	%	%	%	%
Yes – very	42	36	57	57	79
Yes — fairly	24	31	27	23	12
Yes – a little	18	23	10	15	6
Not at all	16	11	6	5	3
Unweighted N	*106*	*235*	*115*	*600*	*96*

Notes:
1. Source: 1998 British Crime Survey.
2. Definition of stalking: persistent and unwanted attention (excluding incidents in which the victim and perpetrator were living with each other throughout the period over which the incidents occurred).
3. Gifts and letters unweighted N too small for reliable analysis.
4. – indicates nil.

Table A6.3: *Impact on lifestyle, by victim typology*

Percentages	Women		Men		All	
	Intimate	Non intimate	Intimate	Non intimate	Intimate	Non intimate
Avoid certain places or people	67	60	56	48	64	57
Extra personal security measures	48	48	12	33	38	44
Go out less often	45	37	26	22	40	33
At least one impact on lifestyle[3]	79	75	60	59	74	71
Unweighted N	*344*	*600*	*110*	*197*	*454*	*797*

Notes:
1. Source: 1998 British Crime Survey.
2. Definition of stalking: persistent and unwanted attention (excluding incidents in which the victim and perpetrator were living with each other throughout the period over which the incidents occurred).
3. Calculated as those victims who said yes to at least one the three impact on lifestyle questions.

Table A6.4:   Impact on lifestyle, by behaviour typology

Percentages	Avoid certain places or people	Go out less often	Take extra personal security measures	At least one mpact on lifestyle[3]	Unweighted N
Silent phone calls	24	14	29	46	106
Followed	52	25	28	61	235
Obscene phone calls	43	31	51	65	115
Violence or threat of violence	72	44	48	83	600
Sexual assault	82	55	49	90	96

Notes:
1. Source: 1998 British Crime Survey.
2. Definition of stalking: persistent and unwanted attention (excluding incidents in which the victim and perpetrator were living with each other throughout the period over which the incidents occurred).
3. Calculated as those victims who said yes to at least one the three impact on lifestyle questions.
4. Gifts and letters unweighted N too small for reliable analysis.

Table A6.5: *Fear of further victimisation, by victim typology*

Percentages	Women		Men		All	
	Intimate	Non intimate	Intimate	Non intimate	Intimate	Non intimate
Afraid violence will/would be used[3]						
Very	14	17	1	13	10	16
Fairly	16	18	16	16	16	18
A little	29	29	16	20	25	27
Not at all	40	36	67	51	49	39
Unweighted N	*210*	*533*	*88*	*151*	*298*	*684*
Afraid violence will/would be used against a relative/friend or someone the victim knew						
Very	19	11	13	19	17	13
Fairly	14	10	15	18	14	12
A little	17	14	15	13	16	14
Not at all	50	65	57	50	52	61
Unweighted N	*344*	*600*	*110*	*197*	*454*	*797*
Afraid a sexual act will/would be committed[4]						
Very	6	12	4	<1	5	9
Fairly	8	15	2	2	6	12
A little	25	24	4	3	19	19
Not at all	61	48	91	95	70	61
Unweighted N	*290*	*566*	*105*	*193*	*395*	*759*

Notes:
1. Source: 1998 British Crime Survey.
2. Definition of stalking: persistent and unwanted attention (excluding incidents in which the victim and perpetrator were living with each other throughout the period over which the incidents occurred).
3. Those victims who reported that the perpetrator had used physical force against them were not asked this question.
4. Those respondents who reported that the perpetrator had forced them into a sexual act against their will were not asked this question.
5. <1 indicates less than 0.5%.

Table A7.1: *Whether the incident was a crime, by victim typology*

	Women		Men		All	
	Intimate	Non intimate	Intimate	Non intimate	Intimate	Non intimate
	%	%	%	%	%	%
A crime	34	33	18	39	30	34
Wrong, but not a crime	38	40	37	29	37	37
Something that just happens	24	21	40	28	29	23
Not sure	4	6	5	4	4	6
Unweighted N	344	600	110	197	454	797

Notes:
1. Source: 1998 British Crime Survey.
2. Definition of stalking: persistent and unwanted attention (excluding incidents in which the victim and perpetrator were living with each other throughout the period over which the incidents occurred).

Table A7.2: *Whether the incident was a crime, by behaviour typology*

	Silent phone calls	Followed	Obscene phone calls	Violence or threat of violence	Sexual assault
	%	%	%	%	%
A crime	30	12	41	37	65
Wrong, but not a crime	44	39	35	37	25
Something that just happens	23	39	16	22	9
Not sure	4	10	7	4	1
Unweighted N	106	235	115	600	96

Notes:
1. Source: 1998 British Crime Survey.
2. Definition of stalking: persistent and unwanted attention (excluding incidents in which the victim and perpetrator were living with each other throughout the period over which the incidents occurred).
3. Gifts and letters unweighted N too small for reliable analysis.

Table A7.3: Whether the police came to know about the incident, by the victim's perceptions of whether their experience was a crime

	A crime	Wrong, but not a crime	Something that just happens
	%	%	%
Police came to know about incident	56	24	18
Police did not know about incident	44	76	82
Unweighted N	439	450	302

Notes:
1. Source: 1998 British Crime Survey.
2. Definition of stalking: persistent and unwanted attention (excluding incidents in which the victim and perpetrator were living with each other throughout the period over which the incidents occurred).
3. 'Not sure' unweighted N too small for reliable analysis.

Table A7.4: Whether the police came to know about the episode of persistent and unwanted attention, by victim typology

	Women		Men		All	
	Intimate	Non intimate	Intimate	Non intimate	Intimate	Non intimate
	%	%	%	%	%	%
Police knew about the incident	31	33	23	38	29	34
Victim reported	23	25	15	24	21	25
Someone else reported	6	6	6	10	6	7
The police knew about it in some other way	2	2	3	4	2	3
Police did not come to know	69	67	77	62	71	66
Unweighted N	344	600	110	197	454	797

Notes:
1. Source: 1998 British Crime Survey.
2. Definition of stalking: persistent and unwanted attention (excluding incidents in which the victim and perpetrator were living with each other throughout the period over which the incidents occurred).

Table A7.5: Whether the police came to know about the episode of persistent and unwanted attention, by behaviour typology

	Silent phone calls	Followed	Obscene phone calls	Violence or threat of violence	Sexual assault
	%	%	%	%	%
Police knew about the incident	30	26	43	36	38
Victim reported	21	17	28	28	26
Someone else reported	5	7	10	6	9
The police knew about it in some other way	3	2	5	1	3
Police did not come to know	70	74	57	64	62
Unweighted N	106	235	115	600	96

Notes:
1. Source: 1998 British Crime Survey.
2. Definition of stalking: persistent and unwanted attention (excluding incidents in which the victim and perpetrator were living with each other throughout the period over which the incidents occurred).
3. Gifts and letters unweighted N too small for reliable analysis.

Table A7.6: Who the victim told, by victim typology

Percentages	Women		Men		All	
	Intimate	Non intimate	Intimate	Non intimate	Intimate	Non intimate
Told someone[3]	83	86	71	74	80	83
Told partner, boyfriend or girlfriend	49	64	31	52	44	61
Told friend, relative or neighbour	73	74	63	65	70	72
Told doctor, social worker or carer	15	5	7	7	13	6
Unweighted N	339	594	107	197	446	791

Notes:
1. Source: 1998 British Crime Survey.
2. Definition of stalking: persistent and unwanted attention (excluding incidents in which the victim and perpetrator were living with each other throughout the period over which the incidents occurred).
3. Includes victim reporting the incident to the police.

Table A7.7: Who the victim told, by behaviour typology

Percentages	Silent phone calls	Followed	Obscene phone calls	Violence or threat of violence	Sexual assault
Told someone[3]	79	78	92	86	71
Told partner, boyfriend or girlfriend	59	47	73	59	39
Told friend, relative or neighbour	66	67	81	76	58
Told doctor, social worker or carer	8	6	5	9	20
Unweighted N	*106*	*232*	*115*	*596*	*96*

Notes:
1. Source: 1998 British Crime Survey.
2. Definition of stalking: persistent and unwanted attention (excluding incidents in which the victim and perpetrator were living with each other throughout the period over which the incidents occurred).
3. Includes victim reporting the incident to the police.
4. Gifts and letters unweighted N too small for reliable analysis.

Appendix B: Developing the behaviour typology

All respondents who said they had experienced persistent and unwanted attention at some point in their lives (since the age of 16) were asked a series of questions to establish what types of behaviour they had experienced. A total of 14 types of behaviour were asked about, ranging from unwanted gifts to sexual coercion (for the full list see Appendix F).

As stated in Chapter 5, most victims experienced more than one type of behaviour during the period of persistent and unwanted attention. Therefore, cluster analysis was used to identify which types of behaviour tended to occur together within episodes.

Cluster analysis

Cluster analysis is a descriptive statistical technique used in the classification of data. The basic aim of cluster analysis is to try and group individuals into meaningful groups. According to Everitt and Dunn (1991) it will provide *"a convenient summary of the multivariate data on which it is based...it will be an aid to memory and the understanding of data"*.

Agglomerative hierarchical clustering techniques are frequently used in data analysis. Essentially this method of clustering is sequential. At each stage the number of groups is reduced by one by joining together, or fusing, the two groups considered to be the most similar, or the closest to each other. Since the clusters at any stage are obtained by the joining together of two clusters from the previous stage, these methods lead to a hierarchical structure.

In order to categorise the data into meaningful clusters a cut off point was decided for the optimum number of clusters needed to explain the data. Obviously the highest level of the hierarchy is the cluster that includes all the observations. However, one large cluster is useless for categorisation. On the other hand using too many clusters will break the data down to such a fine level that no meaningful categories emerge. To decide on the optimum level of detail the most common solution is to examine the dendrogram (a graphical representation of the hierarchical tree structure) for large distances between adjacent fusion levels; such a change from say j to j-1 groups may be indicative of a j cluster solution.

In this instance, both Ward's technique and complete linkage (both agglomerative hierarchical techniques) suggested the same five cluster solution. The only difference between this solution and the final six fold behaviour typology (see Chapter 5) was the cluster analysis suggested the fifth cluster should include both obscene phone calls and forcing the victim into a sexual act against their will (Box B5.1).

As stated earlier cluster analysis is a descriptive technique. There is no 'one solution' and therefore any interpretation is to a degree subjective. By virtue of the seriousness of the different offences, illustrated, for example, by the range of disposals available to the courts and the emotional and physical impact on the victim, the decision was made to separate this cluster into two distinct groups for analysis.

Box B5.1: *Cluster analysis solution and final six-fold behaviour typology:*

Five Cluster Solution	Six Fold Behaviour Typology
Cluster 1 Sending unwanted items: gifts, letters, cards etc Waiting outside place of work/study Refusing to take no for an answer	Type A Gifts and letters
Cluster 2 Silent phone calls	Type B Silent phone calls
Cluster 3 Following Waiting outside home Being forced into talking to the offender	Type C Followed
Cluster 4 Use of physical violence Touching or grabbing Threat of physical violence Physical intimidation	Type D Violence or threat of violence
Cluster 5 Obscene phone calls Forcing victim into a sexual act	Type E Obscene phone calls Type F Sexual assault

Assessing the seriousness of different behaviours

Relative seriousness of each of the six groups was assessed by examining responses to questions on fear of violence, whether the victim perceived the incident to be a crime and the emotional impact of the episode of stalking. The results are given in Tables B5.1 to B5.3. Although the rankings differed slightly between these three measures, the overall patterns were very similar.

The final ranking for the behaviour typology was as follows (from least serious to most):
- Gifts and letters
- Silent phone calls
- Following
- Obscene phone calls
- Violence or threat of violence
- Sexual assault.

Information on how individuals were assigned to one of these six types is given in Chapter 5.

Table B5.1: *Whether the incident was a crime, by type of behaviour experienced*

Behaviour typology	Type of persistent and unwanted attention	Percentage saying it was a crime	Unweighted N
F	Forced victim into a sexual act against their will[3]	65	96
D	Used physical force[3]	60	269
D	Threatened to use violence[3]	59	365
E	Obscene phone calls	46	268
D	Touched or grabbed victim	42	439
D	Physically intimidated victim	42	545
B	Silent phone calls	38	585
C	Waited outside victim's house	37	453
C	Followed victim	36	511
C	Forced to talk to them	34	631
A	Waited outside victim's place of work or study	32	335
A	Refused to take no for an answer	32	429
A	Unwanted items such as gifts	31	255
A	Unwanted letters or cards	27	355

Notes:
1. Source: 1998 British Crime Survey.
2. Definition of stalking: persistent and unwanted attention (excluding incidents in which the victim and perpetrator were living with each other throughout the period over which the incidents occurred).
3. Only those victims who had experienced any of the previous types of persistent and unwanted attention were asked about these three types of behaviour.

Table B5.2: *Emotional impact, by type of behaviour experienced*

Behaviour typology	Type of persistent and unwanted attention	Percentage saying they were very distressed or upset	*Unweighted N*
F	Forced victim into a sexual act against their will[3]	79	*96*
D	Used physical force[3]	74	*269*
D	Threatened to use violence[3]	72	*365*
E	Obscene phone calls	64	*268*
D	Touched or grabbed victim	64	*439*
D	Physically intimidated victim	62	*545*
C	Followed victim	58	*511*
C	Forced to talk to them	57	*631*
C	Waited outside victim's house	57	*453*
B	Silent phone calls	54	*585*
A	Unwanted items such as gifts	53	*255*
A	Refused to take no for an answer	51	*429*
A	Waited outside victim's place of work or study	50	*335*
A	Unwanted letters or cards	46	*355*

Notes:
1. Source: 1998 British Crime Survey.
2. Definition of stalking: persistent and unwanted attention (excluding incidents in which the victim and perpetrator were living with each other throughout the period over which the incidents occurred).
3. Only those victims who had experienced any of the previous types of persistent and unwanted attention were asked about these three types of behaviour.

Table B5.3: Fear of violence, by type of behaviour experienced

Behaviour typology	Type of persistent and unwanted attention	Percentage saying they were very afraid of violence[4]	Unweighted N
D	Threatened to use violence[3]	46	144
E	Obscene phone calls	21	190
D	Physically intimidated victim	20	311
C	Followed victim	18	340
C	Waited outside victim's house	16	298
C	Forced to talk to them	16	451
D	Touched or grabbed victim	15	207
B	Silent phone calls	14	456
A	Refused to take no for an answer	14	309
A	Waited outside victim's place of work or study	13	230
A	Unwanted letters or cards	11	275
A	Unwanted items such as gifts	10	186

Notes:
1. Source: 1998 British Crime Survey.
2. Definition of stalking: persistent and unwanted attention (excluding incidents in which the victim and perpetrator were living with each other throughout the period over which the incidents occurred).
3. Only those victims who had experienced any of the previous types of persistent and unwanted attention were asked about this type of behaviour.
4. Those victims where the offender had used physical force against them were not asked this question.
5. Unweighted N for forcing victim into a sexual act against their will was too small for reliable analysis.

Appendix C: An evaluation of the use and effectiveness of the Protection from Harassment Act: Summary of Home Office Research Study 203 (Harris, 2000)

Background

The Protection from Harassment Act came into force on June 16 1997. One of the Act's aims was to tackle the problem of 'stalking', but it also covered a range of behaviour, which might be classed more broadly as harassment of one kind or other.

The Act introduced two new criminal offences – a section 2 summary offence[49] which deals with conduct that amounts to harassment of another and a section 4 either-way offence[50] that covers situations where the victim fears that violence will be used. For both offences there must be a course of conduct. The court has the power to make a restraining order against those convicted in order to prevent a repetition of the harassment.

When the Act was implemented, the government gave an undertaking to evaluate its success in dealing with cases of harassment. This research was commissioned to evaluate the use and effectiveness of the Act.

Methodology

The study examined 167 Protection from Harassment cases sent by the police to the CPS during 1998 for a decision on prosecution. Using CPS files as the main source of information, details were recorded about the characteristics of each case and its progress through the criminal justice system.

Interviews were also carried out with police officers, Crown Prosecutors, magistrates and victims of harassment.

---

49 Punishable by up to six months in prison or a maximum fine of £5,000 or both.
50 Punishable by up to five years in prison or an unlimited fine or both.

The nature of harassment cases

The study found that the Protection from Harassment Act is being used to deal with a variety of behaviour other than stalking, including domestic and inter-neighbour disputes, and rarely for stalking itself.

- The suspect and victim were known to each other in almost all cases, either as partners, ex-partners or relatives (41% of cases), acquaintances (41%) or neighbours (16%). In only four per cent were the parties strangers.

- The most common reason for harassment was that the complainant had ended an intimate relationship with the suspect.

- Eighty per cent of suspects were male; among victims almost the same proportion were female.

- The study identified several different types of behaviour which constituted harassment. These included:

  - threats (either face-to-face or by telephone)
  - a range of distressing behaviour, such as following the victim, waiting outside their house or making silent telephone calls
  - damaging the victim's property
  - use of violence
  - miscellaneous other actions, such as sending unwelcome gifts or ordering unwanted taxis on the complainant's behalf.

Police action

- Victims usually chose the police as their first port of call when they were subjected to harassment. However, many were unaware of the Act and the remedies available and had endured unwanted behaviour for a significant time before they reported it.

- The police must establish that a course of conduct amounting to harassment has occurred before they can make an arrest. In some cases they might wait until there had been a number of incidents, but in a minority they arrested (incorrectly) when there had apparently only been one.

- In most cases the statement of the victim provided valuable evidence, but it is important that there is corroboration so that the case does not depend only on the victim's word against that of the complainant. Among the important sources of evidence collected by the police were:

  - evidence from other eye-witnesses
  - documentary evidence (e.g. logs of incidents of harassment)
  - material or forensic evidence
  - medical evidence (e.g. of the psychological effect on the victim or of injuries)
  - records of prior police warnings issued to the suspect

- Evidence of previous incidents was not always consistently recorded by the police or readily accessible to other officers who might get called to deal with similar situations involving the same parties.

- The police rarely approached the CPS for advice before charging a suspect. Partly this was because they suspected that the CPS might advise against proceedings but it was also because advice was readily available from senior officers.

- Nationally, roughly three times as many defendants are proceeded against for the less serious section 2 offence as for the section 4 offence. Officers interviewed suggested that it was easier to prove the lower level offence, since they did not have to show that the victim feared that violence would be used. However, they were not always clear as to the difference between the two offences.

- Most suspects charged and bailed (nearly 90%) were given bail conditions – usually designed to prevent them approaching the victim. Only seven per cent were kept in custody for court.

- The officers dealing with cases generally kept victims well informed up to the time of charge, but the provision of information was not always so good after this point. The lack of information at these later stages was felt by some victims to be one aspect of a wider problem of lack of support in helping them through the court process.

The prosecution process and court proceedings

- Thirty-nine per cent of harassment cases were terminated by the CPS, compared with the national average for all offences of 14 per cent (including bindovers). In nearly half of terminated cases the defendant agreed to be bound over. Cases involving neighbour disputes were the most likely to be dropped (nearly half).

- The great majority of terminations were on the grounds of insufficient evidence, most commonly where the victim retracted their complaint.

- Relatively few cases were picked up in which proceedings were dropped because of mental disorder on the part of the suspect. In the few cases where there were grounds to believe that the suspect was mentally disordered, practitioners felt that it was preferable (unless the disorder was severe) to proceed with the case in order to gain access to a restraining order if the case resulted in a conviction.

- As with those given police bail, most defendants bailed by the court were given bail conditions designed to keep them away from the victim. Over 20 per cent were known to have breached their bail conditions. Ten per cent were held in custody after their first court appearance.

- Where cases proceeded to a hearing, 63 per cent of defendants pleaded guilty. Of the remainder, 18 per cent were convicted following a contested trial, while the case against 16 per cent was dismissed. The remaining three per cent were committed to the Crown Court and all were convicted.

- Overall, the conviction rate in cases resulting in a hearing was 84 per cent.

- The sentence most frequently awarded was a conditional discharge (in 43% of convictions). However, this and other sentences were often accompanied by a restraining order (in just over half of convictions).

- Restraining orders were usually specified to run for 12 or 18 months and, like bail conditions, made stipulations designed to stop the offender continuing their harassing behaviour.

- Few breaches of restraining orders were picked up by the research. This was partly due to the limited follow-up period, but it also seems that breaches do occur but are not effectively policed.

Practitioners' views

- Most practitioners interviewed felt that the Protection from Harassment Act is a welcome piece of legislation, enabling intervention in cases of harassment where little could be done before. Magistrates felt confident in dealing with harassment cases – although such cases were not common.

- The most important feature of the legislation was considered to be the restraining order, which was believed to provide protection for the victim. However, for restraining orders to be effective it was felt to be important:
  - to inform victims of the order and its conditions
  - to investigate all the circumstances of the harassment before framing the order
  - to police breaches effectively.

Interviewees identified failings in each of these areas.

- There was some confusion among practitioners about when it was appropriate to use the criminal provisions of the Act rather than the civil remedy. These views were coloured by the perception of some that the Act had originally been introduced to deal with serious cases of stalking rather than domestic or inter-neighbour disputes.

- Among the other issues raised in interviews were:
  - uncertainties among the police about when section 2 and section 4 charges were most appropriate
  - the circumstances in which the police should seek CPS advice before charge
  - the need for further guidance and training in the use of the Act
  - the need to keep victims informed more effectively and support them through the pre-trial and court process.

Conclusions

- The report concludes that the use being made of the Act's criminal provisions is valid but that there is a need to clear up the confusion that exists among practitioners. This might be achieved by issuing some form of guidance or clarification from the centre about what the Act is intended to cover and through enhanced training for all practitioners, as and when opportunities arise.

- In reviewing the effectiveness of the Act, the report notes that the key components are that:
    - the police should pursue appropriate action at the right time
    - victims should be aware of the remedies available to them
    - there should be a rigorous approach to the prosecution of offenders
    - appropriate sentences are passed and executed.

The report draws attention to the need for improvements in each of these areas. Thus:

- for the police, there is a need to be clear about what can be taken to constitute a course of harassment, what proof is required and how best to proceed with a case. The need for training noted above may partly address these issues, but there is also a need to re-examine practices in collecting evidence and in seeking CPS advice;

- in terms of information for victims, there may be a need for greater publicity about the remedies for harassment contained in the Act;

- the high attrition rate of harassment cases points towards the need for greater support for victims during the pre-trial and trial process. But another implication is that only cases suitable for criminal prosecution should be filtered into the criminal process by the police in the first place;

- the operation of restraining orders – effectively the teeth of the Act – needs to be carefully examined. It is surprising that they are not invariably used in harassment convictions. But, more importantly, where they are used they should be framed in a way which is likely to maximise their effectiveness, victims should be aware of the orders and what to do if they are breached, and there should be an effective police and court response to breaches.

Appendix D: The National Violence Against Women Survey

The only large-scale survey apart from the BCS that has produced national level estimates of stalking for men and women is the National Violence Against Women (NVAW) Survey in the United States (Tjaden and Thoennes, 1998).

A question that will inevitably be asked is 'How do the BCS results compare to those from the NVAW Survey?'. The answer to this is that the surveys adopted different methodologies and different definitions of 'stalking' and therefore the results are not comparable. Differences in results between the two surveys should not be taken as evidence of any 'real' difference in the prevalence of 'stalking' between England and Wales and the United States.[51] With this in mind, the results from the two surveys are given in Table D.1.

The NVAW Survey, a telephone survey of adults aged 18 and over, used two definitions of stalking. The first required victims to have felt a high level of fear (to either be 'very' frightened or to have feared that the offender would seriously harm them or someone close to them). The second required only that the victim was somewhat or a little frightened. Relaxing the fear requirement, not surprisingly, resulted in an increase in the estimated prevalence rates. For example the lifetime prevalence among women increased from 8.1 per cent to 12.0 per cent.

The BCS definition was far more inclusive than even the low fear definition used in NVAW Survey, being based on experiences of 'persistent and unwanted attention', regardless of the impact upon the victim. It is therefore not surprising that the BCS prevalence estimates, with the exception of the last year estimate for women, are higher than those from the NVAW Survey. Moreover, it could be surmised that the younger sample in the BCS and the self-completion methodology would also result in higher estimates.

---

51 The only way in which comparisons could be drawn between different countries is for identical surveys, with the same definitions, questions, methods and sample coverage, to be implemented simultaneously in all the countries under consideration. Though even then cultural differences in the willingness to admit to victimisation across different countries will influence the results. See Mayhew and van Dijk, 1997 for a full discussion of these issues in relation to the International Crime Victims Survey.

Table D.1:   The 1998 BCS and 1995/1996 NVAW Survey results

Percentage victims	BCS (England & Wales) No fear requirement	NVAW Survey (United States) High fear definition	NVAW Survey (United States) Low fear definition
Lifetime prevalence			
Women	16.1	8.1	12.0
Men	6.8	2.2	4.0
Last year prevalence			
Women	4.0	1.0	6.0
Men	1.7	0.4	1.5

Notes:
1. Source: 1998 British Crime Survey; 1995/1996 National Violence Against Women Survey.

Although not directly comparable, the results from the two surveys do generally accord with what one would expect given the different methodologies and definitions. However, the higher last year estimate for women in the NVAW Survey is somewhat surprising and may indicate that if the same methodology and definitions had been used in both surveys the rate of stalking would have been higher in the United States.

Appendix E: Survey design and methodological issues

The 1998 sweep of the British Crime Survey was conducted by the National Centre for Social Research (formerly Social and Community Planning Research). The design of the survey, including the stalking self-completion module, was shared between the Research, Development and Statistics Directorate of the Home Office and the National Centre. Previous sweeps were conducted in 1982, 1984, 1988, 1992, 1994 and 1996. The most recent sweep of the survey was conducted in 2000, and the next sweep will be conducted in 2001.[52]

The methodology of the 1998 BCS is discussed below. First, general details of the sample and the interview procedures for both the main face-to-face interview and the stalking self-completion component are given, then methodological issues pertaining to the measurement of stalking victimisation are discussed. For further details about the BCS methodology see Mirrlees-Black et al. (1998) and Hales and Stratford (1999).

The main BCS interview

The majority of the BCS questionnaire is conducted as a face-to-face interview using Computer Assisted Personal Interviewing (CAPI).[53] With CAPI, the questionnaire is a computer program which specifies the questions, the response categories and the routing instructions. Interviewers read the questions and, if appropriate, the response categories, from a computer screen and input the responses directly into a laptop computer during the interview.

The 1998 CAPI questionnaire covered a range of topics including the main crime count (Mirrlees-Black et al., 1998); concern about crime (Mirrlees-Black and Allen, 1998); contacts with and attitudes towards the police (Yeo and Budd, 2000); attitudes to sentencing and the criminal justice system (Mattinson and Mirrlees-Black, 2000); and household security (Budd, 1999).

---

52 From 2001 the BCS will be on an annual, continuous basis with about 40,000 interviews being conducted each year.
53 The BCS has been conducted using CAPI since 1994.

Sample design

The BCS sample is designed to give, after appropriate weighting, a representative sample of adults aged 16 and over living in private households in England and Wales.

A sample of addresses was selected from the Small Users Postcode Address File (PAF) using a stratified multi-stage random probability design.[54] Inner-city areas were over-sampled by a factor of about two. At addresses where there was more than one household, a single household was selected to participate using random selection procedures. At each selected household one adult aged 16 or over was randomly selected for interview. No substitution of respondents was allowed.

Weighting

For analysis purposes the data is weighted to correct for the different probabilities of selection inherent in the sample design. The weighting:

- offsets the over-sampling of inner-city areas
- corrects for cases where there was more than one household at an address
- corrects for cases where there was more than one adult in the household.

Sample size and response rate

A nationally representative sample of 14,947 adults aged 16 and over were successfully interviewed between January and June 1998. The response rate was 79 per cent. The main reasons for non-response at eligible addresses were refusal either by the selected individual (12%) or by the household before the respondent could be selected (1%) and non-contact (4%).

Self-completion modules

The BCS has included a self-completion element since the 1992 sweep, and this has been implemented through CASI (Computer Assisted Self-Interviewing) since 1994.[55]

---

54 The small users PAF is a listing of all postal delivery points in the country which receive less than 25 pieces of mail per day.

55 Not only does CASI result in better data quality than a paper and pencil questionnaire (because respondents can not inadvertently miss questions or enter invalid responses) but evidence from the BCS also suggests that respondents perceive CASI as providing increased confidentiality (Mayhew, 1995).

In the 1998 BCS there were three self-completion modules. The first of these covered drug misuse (Ramsay and Partridge, 1999), the second experience of stalking and the third sexual victimisation.[56] At the end of the CAPI interview respondents aged 16 to 59 were invited to complete the self-completion section.[57] At this point the interviewer passed the laptop computer over to the respondent to allow them to enter their own responses. At the beginning of the self-completion section a screen appeared which provided respondents with guidance about how to enter their responses and instructed them to alert the interviewer if they had any difficulties, for example if they wished to change a response. The method of data entry was kept as simple as possible, with respondents having to press the number which corresponded to their chosen response followed by the 'enter' key, which was indicated by a red sticker.

Response rate

Of the 10,293 respondents aged 16 to 59 in the BCS sample, 97 per cent completed the self-completion module on stalking, either on their own or with assistance. Applying this figure to the main BCS response rate of 79 per cent gives an overall response rate for the stalking self-completion of 76 per cent (this is under the assumption that the response rate among 16-to-59 year-olds was the same as for the sample aged 16 and over). The response rate was similar for men and women (Table E.1).

Table E.1:   Response to the self-completion module

	Men	Women	All
Number of eligible respondents	4,533	5,760	10,293
Refused to complete self-completion	117	188	305
Completed questionnaire[2]	4,416	5,572	9,988
Response rate	97.4	96.7	97.1

Notes:
1. Source: 1998 British Crime Survey.
2. Includes cases in where the interviewer implemented the questionnaire as a face-to-face interview.

The most common reason people gave for refusing to take part was that they 'ran out of time', followed by language problems (Figure E.1).

56 In previous sweeps there have been modules on drug misuse (Mott and Mirrlees-Black, 1995; Ramsay and Spiller, 1997; Ramsay and Percy, 1996); domestic violence (Mirrlees-Black, 1999); sexual victimisation (Percy and Mayhew, 1997) and handling stolen goods (Sutton, 1998).

57 Respondents aged 60 or over are not asked to complete the self-completion because evidence suggests that in general older respondents are less able or willing to complete the self-completion themselves.

Figure E.1:   Reasons for refusing

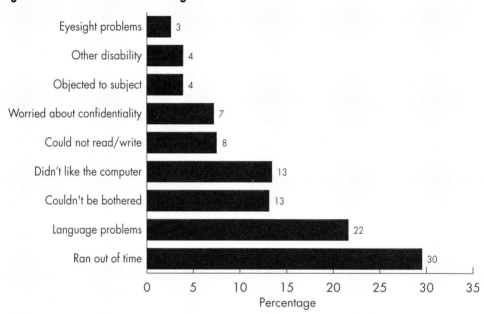

In total, 1,262 respondents who completed the self-completion reported that they had experienced 'persistent and unwanted attention' at some time since the age of 16.

Don't know and refusal codes

Throughout the self-completion questionnaire respondents were permitted to refuse to answer a particular question or answer don't know if they wished to do so. For many questions in the self-completion a refusal option and/or a don't know option were explicitly offered on the screen (see Appendix F). Unless otherwise stated these responses are excluded from the findings presented in this report.

Confidentiality

Self-completion methods have been used in the BCS to collect information which respondents may be reluctant to divulge in a face-to-face interview, either because they do not wish to reveal the information to the interviewer or they do not wish their responses to be overheard by other people present during the interview.

Stalking is a particularly personal crime and therefore it was felt that it would be most appropriate to ask respondents about their experiences in a self-completion module. To maximise the confidentiality afforded by this method, respondents should ideally complete the self-completion modules on their own, without any assistance from the interviewer, in a room in which no-one else, apart from the interviewer, is present.

To reassure respondents of the confidentiality of the exercise, their responses to the self-completion modules were electronically hidden as soon as they had completed the section. This prevented anyone, including the interviewer, gaining access to the data. The data could only be accessed by the research company when it was centrally downloaded.

Presence of others

Interviewers were instructed to try and conduct the interviews, both the face-to-face stage and the self-completion, in private. Unfortunately, this was not always possible to achieve, for various reasons. Table E.2 shows the presence of others during the self-completion modules. Overall, in 33 per cent of cases the self-completion was conducted while someone else was present, most often a spouse or partner. In most of these situations the other person/people in the room did not actually look at or discuss the questionnaire with the respondent. In only 12 per cent of cases where there was someone else present did they become actively involved (4% of all interviews).

Table E.2: *Presence of others during the self-completion module*

	Men	Women	All
No-one else present	3,032 (69%)	3,692 (66%)	6,724 (67%)
Someone else present	1,384 (31%)	1,880 (34%)	3,264 (33%)
Spouse or partner present	859 (19%)	706 (13%)	1,565 (16%)
Adult household member present	282 (6%)	352 (6%)	634 (6%)
Child in household present	143 (3%)	590 (11%)	733 (7%)
Other person present	100 (2%)	232 (4%)	332 (3%)

Notes:
1. Source: 1998 British Crime Survey.

Interviewer assistance

Interviewers were also asked to try and persuade all respondents, who were able to do so, to enter their own responses. In cases in which respondents did not wish to enter their responses or were unable to do so, for example because of eyesight, literacy or dexterity problems, interviewers were permitted to conduct the self-completion as a face-to-face interview, but only if no-one else was present at the time. Overall, five per cent of respondents requested that the interviewer complete the self-completion as a face-to-face interview. In addition a small proportion of respondents who entered their own responses required some assistance from interviewers, for example to change an answer. In these situations interviewers were instructed to try and help by providing instructions for the respondent to follow rather than by directly assisting, and to avoid, if at all possible, looking at the computer screen. The proportion requiring assistance was similar for men and women, but older people required more assistance than younger people (Table E.3, Figure E.2).

Table E.3: **Interviewer assistance on the self-completion module**

	Men	Women	All
Respondent completed self-completion	4,207 (95%)	5,322 (96%)	9,529 (95%)
Without any help	3,965 (90%)	4,927 (88%)	8,892 (89%)
Help with 1 or 2 questions	137 (3%)	239 (4%)	376 (4%)
Help with less than half	24 (1%)	51 (1%)	75 (1%)
Help with more than half	15 (<1%)	26 (<1%)	41 (<1%)
Help with all/nearly all	66 (1%)	79 (1%)	145 (1%)
Interviewer completed	209 (5%)	250 (4%)	459 (5%)

Notes:
1. Source: 1998 British Crime Survey.

Figure E.2: Interviewer assistance by age

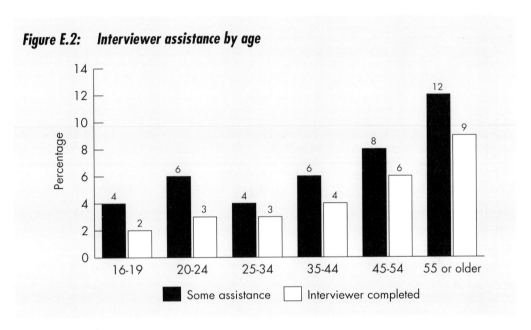

Methodological issues

This section briefly outlines some of the methodological limitations associated with measuring experiences of stalking through a survey self-completion module.

Sampling error

As only a sample of the population was questioned, the estimates will be subject to sampling error. That is, the results may differ to those that would have been obtained if the whole population had been interviewed. The error depends on the size and design of the sample and the size of the estimate. Although, the BCS is large by the standards of most surveys, its estimates will be imprecise. The degree of error is proportionally larger for rarer measures. Tables 2.1 and 7.1 show the 95 per cent confidence intervals on the key estimates.

Due to the stratification and clustering of the BCS sample design, a design factor has to be used when calculating confidence intervals and significance tests. That is, these cannot be calculated on the assumption of a simple random design. The survey company calculates selected design factors. When a specific design factor has not been calculated, as in the case of the questions in this report, the assumption is made that the effective sample size was reduced by a fifth (i.e. a design factor of 1.2). Where used, significance tests have been applied at the 10 per cent level (two tailed).

Coverage

The BCS self-completion modules were asked of a sample of adults aged 16 to 59 who were living in private households in England and Wales. Those aged 60 and over were excluded mainly because the proportion of respondents who complete the self-completion unaided declines among older people (see Figure E.2). Those under the age of 16 are also excluded from the BCS sample, as are those living in institutions or communal establishments and the homeless.

Non response

As in any sample survey, not all those who were eligible to participate actually did so, either because they could not be contacted during the fieldwork period, they refused to take part or were unable do so, for example because of ill health. The response rate for the self-completion module (discussed above) indicates the proportion of the eligible sample who did participate. The failure to include all eligible respondents is only problematic if those who do not participate differ – in terms of the survey measure – to those who do. Although, the BCS response rate is relatively high, certain groups are under-represented, including young men.

Definitions of stalking

Any estimate of stalking is dependent upon the definition of stalking adopted and how it is operationalised.

The BCS self-completion used the term 'persistent and unwanted attention' and gave examples of the types of behaviour that could constitute persistent and unwanted attention. The intention was to have a very broad definition to screen in potential victims. The term 'stalking' was avoided because it has no legal definition and different respondents would interpret the term differently. Moreover, the term 'stalking' has been widely used within the media, focusing on more 'serious' incidents, and this is likely to influence perceptions of what is encompassed by the term. Although, 'persistent and unwanted attention' is not as problematic, inevitably perceptions of what behaviours should be included will vary.

The detailed follow up questions asked of those who did experience persistent and unwanted attention not only throw light on the types of incident that were reported to the survey, but enable various estimates of stalking to be produced based on different definitions.

Response errors

As already discussed the self-completion methodology maximises confidentiality and anonymity and therefore provides more reliable estimates than those obtained from face-to-face interviews. However, the reliability of the estimates still depends upon the ability and willingness of respondents to accurately remember their experiences and report them to the survey. Aside from the definitional problems discussed above there are other sources of response error.

Respondents may simply forget a relevant experience. This is particularly problematic for the lifetime measure, as the longer the recall period the more likely that some incidents, particularly the less serious, will be forgotten.

Despite, the increased confidentiality of self-completion, some respondents may still be reluctant to report their experiences to the survey for a variety of reasons. In some cases respondents may have experienced persistent and unwanted attention but because they do not view what happened as a crime they may be reluctant to mention the incident in a crime survey. This said, the crime context is minimised because the survey does cover a range of issues, including questions about what may be considered as 'marginal' crimes, and the self-completion section is a quite distinct part of the interview process. As demonstrated in Chapter 7, 67 per cent of stalking incidents reported to the survey were not considered to be a crime by the victim.

These response errors are likely to result in an underestimation of the true prevalence of stalking and also to bias the results towards the more serious incidents, though it is not possible to assess the magnitude of the effect.

It should also be borne in mind that in a relatively small proportion of interviews it was not possible for interviewers to implement the self-completion in the ideal way and in these cases the full confidentiality afforded by self-completion was lacking. It is difficult to assess how much of an impact the presence of others or the involvement of the interviewer had on respondents' willingness to report their experiences.

Appendix F   Self-completion questionnaire

Questionnaire asked of all ALL RESPONDENTS AGED 16-59

Square brackets within questions indicates that the text is selected as appropriate given prior answers.

StkIntr1   People may sometimes be pestered or harassed, either by someone they know or a stranger. This person might do things like phoning or writing, following them or waiting outside their home/work place.
                  Cont. Now press 1 and the key with the red sticker to continue)

Stk   [ASK ALL]
                  Since you were sixteen, have you EVER been the subject of such persistent and unwanted attention (from people you know or strangers)?
                  Please include anything you have already told the interviewer about.
                  1.   Yes
                  2.   No
                  3.   Don't want to answer

NumStk   [ASK IF Stk = Yes]
                  How many people carried out this persistent and unwanted attention against you?
                  (If this happened more than once since you were sixteen, please answer about the last person or people who did it)
                  1.   One
                  2.   Two
                  3.   Three
                  4.   More than three
                  5.   Don't know

StkEvCoh   [ASK IF Stk = Yes]
                  Have you ever lived with this person/any of these people?
                  1.   Yes
                  2.   No
                  3.   Don't want to answer

StkWhCoh [ASK IF StkEvCoh = Yes]

Did ALL this persistent and unwanted attention happen while you were living with [this person / any of these people]?

1. Yes
2. No
3. Don't want to answer

StkLiv [ASK IF (StkWhCoh NE Yes) and (StkEvCoh NE No)]

Were you living with [this person/any of these people] at the start of the persistent and unwanted attention?

1. Yes
2. No
3. Don't want to answer

StkIntr3 [ASK IF NumStk = (2-5)]

The next few questions are about the people who carried out the persistent and unwanted attention. If all the pestering was done by everyone in the group, please select one person and answer the questions about this person. Otherwise, please answer about the main person who did it. (Press 1 and the key with the red sticker to continue)

StkSex [ASK ALL]

Was this person...

1. Male
2. Or female
3. Do not want to answer

StkAge [ASK ALL]

At the start of this persistent and unwanted attention, what age was this person? Please make an estimate if you are not sure.

1. Under 16
2. 16-19 (teenage)
3. 20-39 (young adult)
4. 40-59 (middle-aged)
5. 60 or over (older)

WhoStk   [ASK ALL]
            At the start of the persistent and unwanted attention, what was this person's relationship to you?
            1.   [Wife/husband] (now separated)
            2.   Ex - [wife/husband] (now divorced)
            3.   Partner
            4.   Boyfriend/girlfriend
            5.   Someone you went out on a date / a few dates with
            6.   Ex-partner
            7.   Ex-boyfriend/girlfriend
            8.   Other relative
            9.   Other household member
            10.   Someone else you knew
            11.   A stranger

StkRelat   [ASK IF OTHER HH MEMBER OR OTHER RELATIVE]
            Was this person your…
            1.   Parent (including step-parent or in-laws)
            2.   Child (including step-child or in-laws)
            3.   Other relative
            4.   Or non-relative

StkKnw   [ASK IF WhoStk = someone else]
            Was this person your…
            1.   A close friend
            2.   A casual acquaintance
            3.   Employer/manager
            4.   Workmate/colleague
            5.   Doctor/nurse
            6.   Teacher/lecturer
            7.   Client/a member of the public contacted through work
            8.   Landlord/letting agent
            9.   Someone else you knew?

HWWelStk   [ASK IF PARTNER TO SOMEONE ELSE IN WHOSTK]

How well did you know this person at the start of this persistent and unwanted attention?

1.   Know well
2.   Know casually
3.   Know by sight only

StkStHap   [ASK ALL]

Is this persistent and unwanted attention still happening at the moment?

1.   Yes
2.   No
3.   Don't want to answer

StkIntr2   [ASK ALL]

The next few questions are about what this persistent and unwanted attention [has] actually involved.

[Again, please answer about the last main person who did this to you]

(Now press 1 and the key with the red sticker to continue)

HowStk1   [ASK ALL]

[Did/Has] this person ever [send/sent] or [give/given] you unwanted letters or cards?

1.   Yes
2.   No
3.   Don't want to answer

StkNum1   [ASK IF HowStk1 = Yes]

How many times did this happen?

1.   Once
2.   Twice
3.   3-10
4.   11-50
5.   More than 50

HowStk2   [ASK ALL]

[Did/Have] you ever [receive/received] any silent phone calls which you believe were from this person?

1.   Yes
2.   No
3.   Don't want to answer

StkNum2   [ASK IF HowStk2 = Yes]

How many times did this happen?

1.   Once
2.   Twice
3.   3-10
4.   11-50
5.   More than 50

HowStk3   [ASK ALL]

[Did/Has] this person ever [make/made] an obscene phone call to you?

1.   Yes
2.   No
3.   Don't want to answer

StkNum3   [ASK IF HowStk3 = Yes]

How many times did this happen?

1.   Once
2.   Twice
3.   3-10
4.   11-50
5.   More than 50

HowStk4   [ASK ALL]

[Did/Has] this person ever [send/sent] or [give/given] you unwanted items (such as gifts)?

1.   Yes
2.   No
3.   Don't want to answer

StkNum4   [ASK IF HowStk4 = Yes]
How many times did this happen?
1.   Once
2.   Twice
3.   3-10
4.   11-50
5.   More than 50

HowStk5   [ASK ALL]
[Did/Has] this person ever [try/tried] to force you into talking to them?
1.   Yes
2.   No
3.   Don't want to answer

StkNum5   [ASK IF HowStk5 = Yes]
How many times did this happen?
1.   Once
2.   Twice
3.   3-10
4.   11-50
5.   More than 50

HowStk6   [ASK ALL]
[Did/Has] the (last) person who paid you this persistent and unwanted attention ever [follow/followed] you?
1.   Yes
2.   No
3.   Don't know

StkNum6   [ASK IF HowStk6 = Yes]
How many times did this happen?
1.   Once
2.   Twice
3.   3-10
4.   11-50
5.   More than 50

HowStk7   [ASK ALL]
             [Did/Has] this person ever [wait/waited] outside your home?
             1.   Yes
             2.   No
             3.   Don't know

StkNum7   [ASK IF HowStk7 = Yes]
             How many times did this happen?
             1.   Once
             2.   Twice
             3.   3-10
             4.   11-50
             5.   More than 50

HowStk8   [ASK ALL]
             [Did/Has] this person ever [wait/waited] outside your place of
             work/study?
             1.   Yes
             2.   No
             3.   Don't know

StkNum8   [ASK IF HowStk8 = Yes]
             How many times did this happen?
             1.   Once
             2.   Twice
             3.   3-10
             4.   11-50
             5.   More than 50

HowStk9   [ASK ALL]
             [Did/Has] this person [ask/asked] you for a date and [refuse/refused] to
             take no for an answer?
             1.   Yes
             2.   No
             3.   Don't want to answer

StkNum9   [ASK IF HowStk9 = Yes]
                 How many times did this happen?
                 1.   Once
                 2.   Twice
                 3.   3-10
                 4.   11-50
                 5.   More than 50

HowStk10   [ASK ALL]
                 Since the persistent and unwanted attention started, [did/has] this person
                 ever physically [intimidate/intimidated] you (e.g. by cornering you or
                 getting too close?
                 1.   Yes
                 2.   No
                 3.   Don't want to answer

StkNum10   [ASK IF HowStk10 = Yes]
                 How many times did this happen?
                 1.   Once
                 2.   Twice
                 3.   3-10
                 4.   11-50
                 5.   More than 50

HowStk11   [ASK ALL]
                 Since the persistent and unwanted attention started, [did/has] this person
                 ever [touch/touched] or [grab/grabbed] you?
                 1.   Yes
                 2.   No
                 3.   Don't want to answer

StkNum11   [ASK IF HowStk11 = Yes]
                 How many times did this happen?
                 1.   Once
                 2.   Twice
                 3.   3-10
                 4.   11-50
                 5   More than 50

HowStk12   [ASK StkRoute=Yes]
Since the persistent and unwanted attention started [did/has] this person ever   [threaten/threatened] to use violence against you in a way that frightened you?
1.   Yes
2.   No
3.   Don't want to answer

StkNum12   [ASK IF HowStk12 = Yes]
How many times did this happen?
1.   Once
2.   Twice
3.   3-10
4.   11-50
5.   More than 50

HowStk13   [ASK StkRoute=Yes]
Since the persistent and unwanted attention started, [did/has] this person ever [use/used] physical force against you in any way (e.g. by pushing, hitting or kicking you or using a weapon against you)?
1.   Yes
2.   No
3.   Don't want to answer

StkNum13   [ASK IF HowStk13 = Yes]
How many times did this happen?
1.   Once
2.   Twice
3.   3-10
4.   11-50
5.   More than 50

HowStk14   [ASK StkRoute=Yes]
Since the persistent and unwanted attention started, [did/has] this person ever [force/forced] you into a sexual act against your will?
1.   Yes
2.   No
3.   Don't want to answer

StkNum14   [ASK IF HowStk14 = Yes]
              How many times did this happen?
              1   Once
              2.   Twice
              3.   3-10
              4.   11-50
              5.   More than 50

StkLengt   [ASK ALL]
              How long [did/has] the persistent and unwanted attention [go/gone] on
              for in total?
              1.   1 week or less
              2.   More than 1 week, less than 4 weeks
              3.   1 to 3 months
              4.   4 to 5 months
              5.   6 to 11 months
              6.   1 to 2 years
              7.   3 years or more

StkAnn   [ASK ALL]
              [Do/At the time, did] you feel annoyed or irritated?
              1.   Yes - very
              2.   Yes - fairly
              3.   Yes - a little
              4.   Not at all

StkDist   [ASK ALL]
              [Do/At the time, did] you feel distressed or upset?
              1.   Yes - very
              2.   Yes - fairly
              3.   Yes - a little
              4.   Not at all

StkVio   [ASK IF HowStk13 NE Yes]
              [Are/At the time, were] you afraid violence [will/would] be used against you?
              1.   Yes - very
              2.   Yes - fairly
              3.   Yes - a little
              4.   Not at all

StkVioFr   [ASK ALL]

[Are/At the time, were] you afraid violence [will/would] be used against a friend/relative or someone you know?

1.   Yes - very
2.   Yes - fairly
3.   Yes - a little
4.   Not at all

StkSexA   [ASK IF HowStk14 NE Yes]

[Are/At the time, were] you afraid a sexual act [will/would] be committed against you?

1.   Yes - very
2.   Yes - fairly
3.   Yes - a little
4.   Not at all

StkAv   [ASK ALL]

As a result of this experience, [do you/did you at the time] avoid certain places or people?

1.   Yes
2.   No

StkOut   [ASK ALL]

And as a result of this experience, [do you/did you at the time] go out less often than you used to?

1.   Yes
2.   No

StkPrec   [ASK ALL]

Finally, as a result of this experience, [do you/did you at the time] take any extra personal security measures?

1.   Yes
2.   No

Stk1Reas [ASK IF WhoStk IN [Partner...BGFriend]

You said that the [last] person who paid you this persistent and unwanted attention was your current [partner/boyfriend/girlfriend]. Why do you think this person paid you this attention?

1. [He/she] [wants/wanted] to impress me
2. [He/she] [wants/wanted] to upset me
3. Because [he/she] believes [him/herself] to be protecting/guarding me
4. For some other reason
5. Don't know

Stk2Reas [ASK IF WhoStk IN [(ex)husb/wife,date...ex-boy/girlfriend]

You said that the [last] person who paid you this persistent and unwanted attention was [your former spouse/someone you dated/your former partner/your former boyfriend/girlfriend]. Why do you think this person paid you this attention?

1. [He/she] [wants/wanted] to start a relationship
2. Because [he/she] wanted the relationship to continue
3. [He/she] [wants/wanted] revenge/to annoy me now the relationship is over
4. Because [he/she] believes [him/herself] to be protecting/guarding me
5. For some other reason
6. Don't know

Stk3Reas [ASK IF WhoStk IN [Other relative...Stranger]

You said that the [last] person who paid you this persistent and unwanted attention was [a relative/another household member/someone you know/a stranger].

Why do you think this person paid you this attention?

1. [He/she] [wants/wanted] to start a relationship
2. [He/she] [wants/wanted] to annoy or upset me
3. [He/she] [is/was] a CLIENT OR CUSTOMER, demanding service or goods
4. [He/she] [is/was] an EMPLOYER OR COLLEAGUE demanding work
5. [He/she] [wants/wanted] to punish one of my friends or relatives
6. Because [he/she] believes [him/herself] to be protecting/guarding me
7. For some other reason
8. Don't know

StkTell

[ASK ALL]
[Have/At the time it happened, did] you [told/tell] anyone about this persistent and unwanted attention?
1.   Yes
2.   No
3.   Don't want to answer

StkTelPt

[ASK IF StkTell = Yes]
[Did/Have] you [tell/told] a partner/boyfriend/girlfriend [at the time]?
1.   Yes
2.   No

StkTelFr

[ASK IF StkTell = Yes]
[Did/Have] you [tell/told] a friend/relative/neighbour [at the time]?
1.   Yes
2.   No

StkTelDr

[ASK IF StkTell = Yes]
[Did/Have] you [tell/told] a doctor/social worker/carer [at the time]?
1.   Yes
2.   No

StkPol

[ASK ALL]
[Did/Have] the police come to know about the incident?
1.   Yes - I reported it
2.   Yes - Someone else reported it
3.   Yes - They knew in some other way
4.   No

StkSatPl

[ASK IF StkPol = Yes]
Overall, were you satisfied or dissatisfied with the way the police handled this matter?
1.   Very satisfied
2.   Fairly satisfied
3.   A bit dissatisfied
4.   Very dissatisfied
5.   Too early to say

StkWhen   [ASK ALL]
                 Has any of this persistent and unwanted attention taken place in the last
                 year, that is since [Month/Year]?
                 1.   Yes
                 2.   No

VicAge   [ASK IF StkWhen = No]
                 How old were you when this last happened?
                 16..97

StkCrime   [ASK ALL]
                 Do you think what happened was...
                 1.   ...a crime
                 2.   ...wrong, but not a crime
                 3.   ...just something that happens
                 4.   ...or not sure?

StkElse[58]   [ASK ALL]
                 Apart from this, have you ever experienced persistent and unwanted
                 attention from anyone else?
                 1.   Yes
                 2.   No

QSelfCom   Please tell the interviewer you have finished this section.
                 He/she needs to press a key to continue with the next section
                 0.   Skip
                 1.   Continue

---

58 The data pertaining to the variable StkElse was unfortunately not saved by the CAPI program, hence analysis for
    this variable is not possible.

References

Australian Bureau of Statistics (1996). *Women's Safety, Australia, 1996.* Canberra: Commonwealth of Australia.

Brown, H. (2000). *Stalking and other forms of harassment: An investigators guide.* Police Research Award Scheme.

Buck, W., Chatterton, M. and Pease, K. (1995). *Obscene, threatening and other troublesome telephone calls to women in England and Wales: 1982-1992.* Research and Planning Unit Paper 92. London: Home Office.

Budd, T. (1999). *Burglary of Domestic Dwellings: Findings from the British Crime Survey.* Home Office Statistical Bulletin 4/99. London: Research, Development and Statistics Directorate.

Campbell, K. (1997/98). Stalking around the main issue. *Kings College Law Journal,* 8: 128-133.

Coleman, F. L. (1997). Stalking Behaviour and the Cycle of Domestic Violence. *Journal of Interpersonal Violence,* 12, 3:420-432.

Everitt, S. and Dunn, G. (1991). *Applied Multivaribale Data Analysis.* London: Edward Arnold.

Farnham, F. R., James D. V. and Cantrell, P. (2000). Association between violence, psychosis, and relationship to victim in stalkers. *Lancet 2000, 355,* 9199.

Hales, J. and Stratford, N. (1999). *1998 British Crime Survey Technical Report.* London: Social and Community Planning Research.

Hall, D. M. (1998). The victims of stalking. In J. R. Meloy (ed), *The Psychology of Stalking* (pp. 113-137). San Diego, CA: Academic Press.

Harris, J. (2000). *An evaluation of the use and effectiveness of the Protection from Harassment Act.* Home Office Research Study No. 203. London: Home Office.

Hough, M. (1995). *Anxiety about Crime: Findings from the 1994 British Crime Survey.* Home Office Research Study No. 147. London: Home Office.

Kershaw, C., Mayhew, P., Budd, T., Kinshott, G., Mattinson, J. and Myhill, A. (forthcoming) *The 2000 British Crime Survey: England and Wales.* Home Office Statistical Bulletin. London: Research, Development and Statistics Directorate.

Marston, J. and Thompson, K. (1997). Protection from Harassment Act 1997. *Justice of the Peace and Local Government Law,* August 2nd.

Mattinson, J. and Mirrlees-Black, C. (2000). *Attitudes to Crime and Criminal Justice: Findings from the 1998 British Crime Survey.* Home Office Research Study No. 200. London: Home Office.

Mayhew, P. (1995). Some methodological issues in crime victimisation surveys. *Crime Victim Surveys in Australia – Conference Proceedings.* Brisbane: Criminal Justice Commission.

Mayhew, P. and van Dijk, J. J. M. (1997) *Criminal Victimisation in Eleven Industrialised Countries: Key findings from the 1996 International Crime Victims Survey.* Onderzoek en beleid 162; Justitie Wetenschappelijk Onderzoek – en Documentatiecentrum.

Meloy, J. R. (1998). The psychology of stalking. In J. R. Meloy (ed), *The Psychology of Stalking* (pp. 2-24). San Diego, CA: Academic Press.

Mirrlees-Black, C. (1999). *Domestic Violence: Findings from a new British Crime Survey self-completion questionnaire.* Home Office Research Study No. 191. London: Home Office.

Mirrlees-Black, C., Budd, T., Partridge, S. and Mayhew, P. (1998). *The 1998 British Crime Survey: England and Wales.* Home Office Statistical Bulletin 21/98. London: Research, Development and Statistics Directorate.

Mirrlees-Black, C. and Allen, J. (1998). *Concern about Crime: Findings from the 1998 British Crime Survey.* Research Findings No. 60. London: Home Office.

Mirrlees-Black, C., Mayhew, P. and Percy, A. (1996). *The 1996 British Crime Survey: England and Wales.* Home Office Statistical Bulletin 19/96. London: Research and Statistics Directorate.

Mott, J. and Mirrlees-Black, C. (1995). *Self-reported Drug Misuse in England and Wales: Findings from the 1992 British Crime Survey.* Research and Planning Unit Paper 89. London: Home Office.

Mullen, P. E., Pathé, M. and Purcell, R. (2000). *Stalkers and their victims.* Cambridge: Cambridge university Press.

Nicastro, A. M., Cousins, A. V. and Spitzberg, B. H. (2000). The tactical face of stalking. *Journal of Criminal Justice,* 28, 69-82.

Pathé, M. and Mullen, P. E. (1997). The impact of stalkers on their victims. *British Journal of Psychiatry,* 170: 12-17.

Percy, A. and Mayhew, P. (1997). Estimating sexual victimisation in a National Crime Survey: A new approach. *Studies on Crime and Crime Prevention* Vol. 6., No. 2 pp125-150.

Ramsay, M. and Percy, A. (1996) *Drug misuse declared: results of the 1994 British Crime Survey.* Home Office Research Study No. 151. London: Home Office.

Ramsay, M. and Spiller, J. (1997) *Drug misuse declared in 1996: Latest results from the British Crime Survey.* Home Office Research Study No. 172. London: Home Office.

Ramsay, M. and Partridge, S. (1999) *Drug Misuse Declared in 1998: results from the British Crime Survey.* Home Office Research Study No. 197. London: Home Office.

Roberts, A. R. and Dziegielewski, S. F. (1996). Assessment typology and intervention with survivors of stalking. *Aggression and Violent Behaviour.* Winter 1, 4: 359-368.

Sheridan, L., Davies, G.M. and Boon, J. (forthcoming). *Stalking: Perceptions and Prevalence.* Journal of Interpersonal Violence.

Sutton, M. (1998). *Handling stolen goods and theft: A market reduction approach.* Home Office Research Study No. 178. London: Home Office.

Tjaden, P. and Thoennes, N. (1998). *Stalking in America: Findings from the National Violence Against Women Survey.* Washington D.C.: U.S. Department of Justice.

Wallis, M. (1996). Outlawing Stalkers. *Policing Today,* 2, 4: 25-29.

Wright, J. A., Burgess, A. G., Laszlo, A. T., McCrary, G. O. and Douglas, J. E. (1996). A Typology of Interpersonal Stalking. *Journal of Interpersonal Violence,* 11, 4:487-502.

Yeo, H. and Budd, T. (2000). *Policing and the Public: Findings from the 1998 British Crime Survey*. Research Findings No. 113. London: Home Office.

RDS Publications

Requests for Publications

Copies of our publications and a list of those currently available may be obtained from:

Home Office
Research, Development and Statistics Directorate
Communications Development Unit
Room 201, Home Office
50 Queen Anne's Gate
London SW1H 9AT
Telephone: 020 7273 2084 (answerphone outside of office hours)
Facsimile: 020 7222 0211
E-mail: publications.rds@homeoffice.gsi.gov.uk

alternatively

why not visit the RDS web-site at
Internet: http://www.homeoffice.gov.uk/rds/index.htm

where many of our publications are available to be read on screen or downloaded for printing.